Turnaround Journey

Discovering a Path for Effective Church Leadership

George L. Yates

TURNAROUND
JOURNEY

Discovering a Path for Effective
Church Leadership

GEORGE L. YATES

PUBLISHING

Belleville, Ontario, Canada

TURNAROUND JOURNEY: DISCOVERING A PATH FOR
EFFECTIVE CHURCH LEADERSHIP
Copyright © 2015, George L. Yates

All Scripture quotations, unless otherwise specified, are from the Holman Christian Standard Bible ® Copyright © 2003, 2002, 2000, 1999 by Holman Bible Publishers. All rights reserved.

Scripture quotations marked KJV are from *The Holy Bible, King James Version.* Copyright © 1977, 1984, Thomas Nelson Inc., Publishers.

Cataloguing data available from Library and Archives Canada

ISBN: 978-1-4600-0452-4
LSI Edition: 978-1-4600-0453-1
E-book ISBN: 978-1-4600-0454-8
(E-book available from the Kindle Store, KOBO and the iBooks Store)

For more information, please contact:
SonC.A.R.E. Ministries
soncare.net
Essence Publishing is a Christian Book Publisher dedicated to furthering the work of Christ through the written word. For more information, contact:

20 Hanna Court, Belleville, Ontario, Canada K8P 5J2
Phone: 1-800-238-6376. Fax: (613) 962-3055
Email: info@essence-publishing.com
Web site: www.essence-publishing.com

Printed in Canada
by

Essence
PUBLISHING

Contents

Introduction

Moses was a leader chosen by God. In the book of Exodus, we read of his experience leading, mainly leading the Israelite nation from captivity on a forty-year journey in the wilderness before they would enter the Promised Land. A leader chosen by God to lead His people, yet a leader who needed development. Though God gave Moses this monumental task, God did not give him every facet of expert leadership ability. Instead God placed around Moses others with complementary personalities and leadership skills. Moses had Aaron and Miriam and later Joshua and others.

Exodus chapter eighteen tells us of one lesson in leadership for Moses from an unlikely source.

> Moses' father-in-law Jethro, along with Moses' wife and sons, came to him in the wilderness where he was camped at the mountain of God. He sent word to Moses, "I, your father-in-law Jethro, am coming to you with your wife and her two sons."
>
> …The next day Moses sat down to judge the people, and they stood around Moses from morning until evening. When Moses' father-in-law saw everything he was doing for them he asked, "What is this thing you're doing for the people? Why are you alone sitting as judge, while all the people stand around you from morning until evening?" Moses replied to his father-in-law, "Because the people come to me to inquire of God. Whenever they have a dispute, it comes to me, and I make a decision between one man and another. I teach them God's statutes and laws."
>
> "What you're doing is not good," Moses' father-in-law said to him. "You will certainly wear out both yourself and these people who are with you, because the task is too heavy for you. You can't do it alone. Now listen to me; I will give you some advice, and God be with you. You be the one to represent the people before God and bring their cases to Him. Instruct them about the

statutes and laws, and teach them the way to live and what they must do. But you should select from all the people able men, God-fearing, trustworthy, and hating bribes. Place them over the people as commanders of thousands, hundreds, fifties, and tens. They should judge the people at all times. Then they can bring you every important case but judge every minor case themselves. In this way you will lighten your load, and they will bear it with you. If you do this, and God so directs you, you will be able to endure, and also all these people will be able to go home satisfied" (Exodus 18:5-6, 13-23 HCSB).

Moses had the daunting task of leading God's people, yet God did not give Moses all the ability, skill, and gifts needed to be the sole person responsible for leadership and administration. Neither did God extend the day for Moses to have enough time to solely take on the task. Moses needed to share the responsibility of leadership and trust God that all would be okay. Moses' greatest need was not necessarily skill but the need to recognize effective deployment of leadership and implementation of God's plans. Moses was attempting to manage people and all their predicaments instead of leading the Israelite nation.

The same is true for you and me today. Whether you are a pastor, a teacher of a Sunday school class, or a leader of any ministry group or organization outside the church, God has placed around you complementary personalities with complementary gifts and skills. Do not try to be Superman or the Lone Ranger because that is not who God created you to be.

In ministry, one of the difficulties we face is implementation. I realize some churches have difficulty in effective planning. This is why in *Reaching the Summit: Avoiding and Reversing Decline in the Church,* I strongly recommend that a church use an experienced, trained outside observer—a coach to help lead you through planning and the transitions of implementation. A coach is not someone who will come in and give you the four steps to success. Rather a coach guides you as a ministry to discover and develop the gifts, talents, and skills God has already blessed and placed within your ministry. Effective implementation of a strategic plan is critical for any level of success.

The men whom Jethro referred to were right there in the same camp with Moses. Moses simply had not recognized them. Moses was trying to manage instead of lead. Jethro's suggestion was for Moses to change and become the leader these people needed and not the manager he had become. I do not know of one person who ever entered ministry to be a manager. We follow God's calling into ministry to lead: to lead people to faith in Christ, to lead people into maturing disciples, to lead people to lead others. Yet too often we find ourselves managing instead of leading, just as had happened to Moses. Many pastors and ministers are managing programs, people, and facilities instead of leading people.

Every leader needs to discover those persons God has placed in our midst with complementary personalities and skills. We must learn to utilize these persons and trust God to use them in assisting in the planning and implementation phases. Without proper planning, even the best of plans will fall short of success. And of course this all begins with prayer and must be bathed in prayer throughout the process.

As you read this book, my prayer is that you will be open to the Holy Spirit of God reaching inside you and leading you on a discovery path of your own leadership practices, growing in you a desire to reach for your full potential of leadership in all areas of life. Everyone reading this book has multiple circles of influence and leadership: at work, at home as a parent, husband, or wife, in the church, and in all other circles of influence given to you by our great God. Learn the principles in this book on leadership and implementation, and you will see the principles overlap into every area of your life.

Each chapter in this book tells part of a story of one church's leaders and their journey for implementation. Following the story portion, each chapter will give you direct insights from that chapter for particular implementation or leadership characteristics in a **Debrief** section. In other words, in each chapter you will receive part of the story and a description of why and how to implement certain aspects in your own ministry (and life).

Whether you pastor a church or work in the corporate world, whether you lead a multi-staff church or you are the only paid staff person, the principles and leadership characteristics can be applied in your situation. While this work is written with ministry leaders in mind, even before it has been published, I have had corporate executives write to tell me they are adopting some of these principles in their business leadership. Principles are principles, and they cross over into other areas of life as well.

I have not written this story in a vacuum thinking it is a perfect situation and non-stressful life at this particular church. However, I also did not write about the tensions and stress coming from the whirlwind busy schedules of pastors and church staff. Certainly the pastor and staff faced trials and objections to change as is common in churches and other organizations. Certainly there are the change resistors in this church as perhaps are in yours. Instead of drawing out those conflicts and stress points, I chose to focus on the principles and practices that will assist you in prayerfully considering and developing a strategic plan of progress as well as implementation processes to move your church to God's desired and focused operation. The original premise of this book was to give leaders a prescription for building strategic plans and implementation processes. In addition, you will read of thirty-three practices and principles to increase the effectiveness of your leadership while nurturing leaders and followers within your influence.

While you may read this book from cover to cover as a novel or an educational work, you will best be served by reading it chapter by chapter. Stopping at the close of each chapter to consider the principles of leadership and practices portrayed in the story and described in the Debrief section will allow you to work through and grow in your leadership skills. The very best application will be to read and study through this work for your own personal interest first. Then follow through by taking your staff, lay leaders, or a group of your peers through this material. Taking your staff or leadership team through this will strengthen your team in approach, desire, skill, and cooperation as well as giving you a well-prepared strategy for planning and implementing vision and goals. Doing so will build solid leaders and give a formula for strategic planning and implementation for any and all levels within your organization.

Our Story

Reverend Tim Farling is the pastor of Calvert City Community Church, conveniently known to its members as 4Cs. Tim accepted the position of pastor eighteen months prior to where our story begins. He has had previous experience pastoring a church, and his previous church (Bethany Neighborhood Church) tripled in size in seven years. Tim and his wife, Leigh Ann, both believe this was God's call on Tim's life to lead 4Cs, and he has not doubted that calling in his short tenure with the church. However, he did not expect some of the difficulty the church has faced.

Tim's first church—at least it seemed so looking back—had almost grown on auto-pilot, well, at least once the wheels were turning. Tim has spent several evenings the last few weeks contemplating the situation at 4Cs, trying to find comparisons between 4Cs and his first church; looking for potential and possibilities for stopping—no, reversing—the declining trends this church has been experiencing for the past ten years. At times it seemed like the decline had slowed and they were adding people to their attendance and membership. "Certainly that is a good sign, right?" Every time that thought passes through his head, Tim reminds himself, "Or could it be because I'm new, we've just come out of the honeymoon phase?" The honeymoon phase is a term used to describe a new pastor's first months on the field as pastor—a time when pastor and members are getting to know one another and not much change is made. People accept each other without dissent, attempting to learn the traits and quirks of one another during the honeymoon period. However, once the honeymoon is over, people seem to change.

Tim naturally is concerned. Concerned that if things do not turn around, could he lose his job? Will members of the church ask him to leave as they did their previous pastor? Whether or not that is the case, his other concerns are just as viable: will there be enough money to budget for the ministries next year, and what about staff? If financial resources fall off much more, will he need to let staff go and move to part-time or volunteer staff positions? If decline continues, will he have enough people to staff the on-going ministries? What ministries will suffer and need to be scaled back or eliminated?

Tim enjoys working with his staff and believes they make a good team for serving 4Cs. There are four other paid staff members. Roger Wilson is Worship Pastor. Roger is nearing his five-year anniversary with 4Cs and seems to have a good rapport with the lay leaders and members of the church.

Andy Graeter is the church's Student Minister, responsible for ministry and discipleship of all students from fifth grade through college years. Andy is the newest member of the staff, having joined the church staff just over a year prior to our story's beginning.

Marcy Yeager is a part-time staff person serving in the children's and preschool areas for the church. Marcy and her family joined 4Cs church when she was a freshman in high school. Now married with two children of her own, Marcy is a vital team member coordinating the ministries for preschool and children's ages through fourth grade.

The fifth member of the staff is Susan Tompkins, the Administrative Assistant. Susan is the first point of contact in the church office and is responsible for phone reception, church print publications, managing office volunteers, and other office clerical duties.

As the story progresses, you will be introduced to other characters. But for now, these are the paid staff members and the team leading the church at this point in its history.

Three months prior to where we pick up the story, Tim and 4Cs had brought in a denominational leader to assist them in unearthing the reality of their situation. Tim realized everyone in the church, including himself as pastor, would always look at the church with a particular bias. Therefore, they could not possibly come to an unbiased conclusion of the reality of their situation. Having an experienced and objective observer from outside the church was the only way 4Cs could reach a balanced and detached assessment.

The denominational consultant had led the church through a series of meetings in an intense investigation of the true facts (sometimes brutal facts) of the reality of the church's current situation. To Tim and some in the church, it was truly an eye-opening experience. Some were shocked at the findings, while others were in denial about the findings and the need for change. The main conclusion from this vigorous face-to-face summit with reality was the need to change—and not for the sake of change.

The facts proved that 4Cs had been losing members and resources for at least ten years. In addition to this, the church members had become a turned-inward societal group. In other words, most of what they were doing as a church was for the current members and not reaching others outside the church. Another conclusion coming out of this inward-turned mentality was that the church had experienced little to no spiritual growth, which was encumbering them from reaching others and carrying out God's ministry plan—the Great Commission.

Tim is not the only pastor who ever faced these issues, and likely he will not be the last. Let's follow Tim on this *Turn-Around Journey,* as he has expressively named it, for the situation of 4Cs church.

Chapter 1

The Staff Meeting

Confident of what he is about to introduce, yet hesitant, Pastor Tim gathers his notes and pen and leaving his office, heads down the hall to the meeting room. When he arrives, the worship pastor, Roger, and Marcy, the children's ministry director, are already seated at the table ready for the staff meeting to begin. The three exchange greetings. As Pastor Tim makes his way to his regular seat at the opposite end of the room, his administrative assistant, Susan, walks into the room and claims, "Sorry, I was on the phone with Deacon Ellis."

"No problem," Roger responds. "We haven't started yet, and besides, Andy [the church's student pastor] isn't here yet either." Looking at his watch, Roger adds, "It's not time for him yet." Marcy and Susan share a chuckle with Roger. They all know Andy always walks in at the last minute as the weekly staff meetings are about to start—sometimes he's even later, arriving after the meeting begins. But it is not only staff meetings. Andy is always cutting it to the last minute to arrive for any meeting.

Just as the clock on the wall clicks over to 10:00, in scurries Andy. "Right on time," remarks Roger, and everyone seated has another chuckle.

Looking surprised at the comment, Andy replies, "What, am I late?"

Roger retorts with a twist of the head from right to left, "No, you're right on time, like I said."

Even Pastor Tim smiles and says, "Let's begin. Roger, I believe you have our devotion this morning." Roger nods and begins sharing a five-minute devotion and challenge to the staff about their personal prayer life, then leads the group in prayer.

"Thanks, Roger," says Tim. "Susan, what's on our calendar for the next four weeks?" As Administrative Assistant, one of Susan's duties is to coordinate the church activities calendar and keep the staff abreast of all updates. Susan begins reading the upcoming ministry events and activities, allowing time for discussion for each one. This part of the weekly meeting is almost routine. Susan calls off each event on the calendar, and each staff member gives an update for the planning and implementation progress of each activity in his or her ministry area. Today, the calendar discussion carries on for fifteen minutes.

"Good. Now what else do you have for us?" Looking around the table, Tim asks the question for everyone. "Marcy, you first this week." Marcy shares first, then each of the other staff members take a turn, each one taking about two minutes to share. (**Debrief:** *Two-Minute Report*) One at a time, each member shares what is on his or her plate for the upcoming week: special projects, time out of the office, staffing issues, all the major things that will be occupying his or her time for the coming week. The team has worked on this to streamline meetings and make effective use of their meeting time. It also keeps everyone updated with each one's activities within their respective ministries. If there is something that needs attention, the team will address it. However, these discussions will come after everyone has completed their two-minute report. For instance, last week, Marcy asked for advice on approaching one of her preschool volunteers about punctuality. In this situation, Pastor Tim calls for input from the other staff members before weighing in himself.

Pastor Tim has learned to wait and gather input from everyone else in any meeting before commenting. Otherwise, he knows most church members and volunteers are likely to agree with the pastor, and the team may miss out on some very good input and possibly the best solution. It is not that all church members are "yes" men and women. But in church life, once the pastor speaks, it is often common practice to agree with the pastor's comments and analogy. (**Debrief:** *Leader's Input Comes Last*)

This week, no issues have arisen, and in ten minutes, everyone has had their time to share what's pressing in each ministry area. It is now 10:30, and everyone is up to date on the calendar and the schedules of each ministry leader for the week, as well as the opening devotion and prayer. Things are moving along fine, and Pastor Tim thinks to himself, *"Now, to get through the rest of the meeting with as much speed, focus, and clarity."*

Pastor Tim speaks up to keep the meeting moving along, "Well, you know my first two questions." They're the same every week. "What did we do right this weekend?" referring to the worship services and overall flow of the church's weekend experience.

Marcy speaks up first, "I loved the special music and thought the worship experience was very personable this week."

Roger gives a nod of thanks as Andy joins right in, "Yes, I thought the music and scripture tied in well with your [looking at Tim] message and helped people to have personal worship."

This went on for a couple of minutes before Tim asked, "Okay the second question, What could we have improved upon?" Silence. Unless there was something obvious in the service, like a sound board malfunction, this question every week brings a silent pause with everyone looking down at their notes or the table in front of them. Sometimes Pastor Tim will throw out a question to spark conversation such as, "What are your thoughts on..." Other times, like today, silence prevails.

"Okay," says Tim after about thirty seconds of silence, which of course to everyone feels like ten minutes. "I have something new to talk about this morning for the remainder of our meeting. We are not going to finish this today, but I want us to get a good start, dialoguing about it." The staff and a few others have recently completed a Vigorous Face-to-Face Summit with Reality,[1] an intense examination of the reality of the church's situation. For more information about the Vigorous Face-to-Face Summit with Reality, read chapter seven of *Reaching the Summit: Avoiding and Reversing Decline in the Church.*

Tim continues, "I have been thinking about our next steps, having finished our assessments and reality check last month. With all the information we gleaned from that process, we have much that we can work on and consider to improve how we 'do church.'" Heads are nodding around the table, remembering the discussions from the last three months of reviewing assessments, questionnaires, historical data, and their vigorous face-to-face summit with reality—a real facing of the brutal facts of the reality of the situation of the church.

Then all eyes turn back to Tim as he continues: "We have all agreed that the information we learned through that process is very helpful and eye opening for us in realizing where the church really is and how to improve. However, if we never do anything more about it and only consider it good information, it has done us no good at all. We will be no better off than we were before all that time assessing our situation if we do nothing with what we have learned through it."

"Absolutely," chimes in Roger, though the tone in his voice isn't as reassuring as his words.

"I think I like where this might be headed," says Andy, the forever risk-taking, forward-thinking, younger member of the group.

With an air of hesitation in both her voice and words, Marcy replies to Andy's enthusiasm, "I...I'm not certain I'm comfortable with this yet. Tell us more, Pastor." (Debrief: *Marcy's Hesitation*)

Tim gives a small smile as he continues, "If we are going to completely turn this thing around and make needed adjustments, we need a plan of execution. We need a strategic implementation plan. We need a nuts-and-bolts plan of how to make the needed adjustments."

"You're talking about change," spouts Roger, "We need to be careful, or it might just be our own execution we're planning." A smile crosses the face of everyone in the room at the play on words from Roger. Well, everyone except Marcy, that is. She grimaces and gives a squeamish nod.

"It's not going to be easy, and it will take some time," Tim asserts. "But our church did not get in this situation overnight. We've all gotten comfortable, and as we found out in our assessment, we have slipped away from our main purpose. Not intentionally, but we have let the whirlwind of life distract us in many areas. We all agreed last month that we need to realign ourselves, our ministries, and all our efforts to be more effective. The natural next step is to begin planning a process that will help us accomplish that feat. Wouldn't you agree?"

Nods come from every head around the table. Andy is the first to speak, "Absolutely! And the sooner the better." Andy's quick-start enthusiasm shines through.

"Hang on just a minute there, Andy," responds Roger. "Patience is a virtue. I heard Tim say it is going to take some time. It's not something we need to rush into."

"Yeah, but..." Andy retorts, "I don't want us to lose this motivation to move the ministry forward. The longer we wait, the more opportunities we will miss. I'm ready to go now. Let's get started."

"Roger is right," Tim interjects. "This is not something we can jump into or make quick, rash decisions. We need to be deliberate in seeking the right path and the right means to move this train down the track. At the same time, I appreciate and understand your eagerness. I too am eager to see this ministry once again flourishing. However, one of the greatest things we can do for this church, ourselves, and God is to *pace our change*."

"And prayer," adds Susan, who has been quiet throughout this discussion. She adds, "It seems to me prayer needs to be at the top of our list, too."

Everyone is nodding in agreement. "Good. Thank you, Susan," responds Tim. "That leads me to my next point. It's like you read my notes and gave me a perfect segue." Smiles and quiet laughter come from around the table. Tim continues, "No matter what we do or plan, it is all futile without prayer. And I'm not talking prayer as usual. Every part of this, every meeting, every idea, and every practice must be bathed in prayer. Perhaps the first change we need is the way we pray."

"What do you mean," asks Roger.

"Well, I want us to be intentional about prayer. And more than intentional, we need to get our other leaders in the church together and study prayer. Then we need to practice thorough, intensive prayer in our lives and the way we lead the church in prayer. To be effective, we must bathe every decision and every action in prayer." (Debrief: *Bathed in Intentional Prayer*)

Everyone in the room knows Pastor Tim is right. "Too often our prayer lives become routine. Even the prayers we say in church are often more routine than heartfelt," says Marcy. "No offense intended."

Tim lets out almost a shout of exclamation. "That's exactly what I'm talking about. Thanks, Marcy." He knows Marcy understands what he is trying to say. The others seemed to all agree with nods and a couple of humble and quiet "yes" responses. "Too often our prayers are routine and cliché. We pray, 'bless me, Lord,' 'bless the gift and the giver,' 'lead, guide, and direct us,' and 'put a hedge of protection around us.' While some of these may be good prayers, we're praying them because we heard someone else pray them. We are praying more from our head than from our heart. We need to change this."

Tim then issues the challenge. "If we are going to make this a matter of prayer and prayer is to be most important, then let's start now! I will begin, then you all can pray as well. Roger, you close us after everyone has had the opportunity." Tim paused, then said, "Pray from your heart, as Marcy suggested. Don't worry about the time, we've got all day."

Actually, Tim and Roger have a lunch engagement, and Andy needs to be at his daughter's school at 12:30. But they all know what Tim means by his "all day" comment. If God is leading us to continue to pray, let's pray. Do not let the clock get in the way.

Tim begins: "God in Heaven, I come to You this morning with a humble heart. We are Your leaders here at Calvert City Community

Church, and we, first and foremost, must accept responsibility for the situation this church finds itself in. It is our watch, and we are responsible for leading and equipping Your church to fulfill its purpose and mission—the Great Commission. You have gifted each one of us and brought us here at this time in history for a reason. Help us each one to seek out that reason every day as You bless us and give us breath. I am, we are, truly repentant for not coming to You before now, more fervently, asking forgiveness and seeking Your perfect will for this church. As we begin this planning process, guide us in every thought, idea, ministry effort, and planning stage. Then lead us through the implementation process only as you would have us proceed..." Tim continues his prayer, asking God to bring to the forefront the special gifts and strengths of each staff team member. Each one in the room follows with their own prayer for themselves, each other, and the church.

When Roger closes the prayer, Tim looks at the clock on the wall and says, "11:50. When we set our hearts on God and do not let the distractions of life get in the way, look what we can do." To everyone's astonishment, they had just spent fifty minutes with heads bowed praying. *"It didn't seem that long,"* Marcy thinks to herself. Looking around the table, she can tell the others all have similar thoughts running through their heads, and expressions of humble satisfaction adorn each face.

Following a short pause of silence as each one ponders what they had just experienced, Tim adds, "We've got just a few minutes left, so let's do this. This next week let's each one think of—and pray about—ways we can lead our church in effective prayer emphases for the future of this church. Everyone come back next week with at least two ideas to propose. We'll compile the list, discuss each one, come up with two to three to begin with, and move forward from there. Thanks, team. Let's go out in God's grace."

The meeting is dismissed and everyone, gathering notebooks, water bottles, and coffee mugs, heads out the door. Roger and Marcy engage in small talk as they leave the room, walking down the hall to their offices. Andy checks his phone and begins humming a tune as he exits. Tim and Susan are the last to leave the room. As they get to the door, Tim snaps his fingers as if he has just remembered something, and he looks at Susan to say, "Remind me when I get back from lunch to send an e-mail to everyone [meaning the staff] about our focus." Susan jots something on her notepad as they walk down the hallway.

DEBRIEF

TWO-MINUTE REPORT

The challenge (at first implementing this) is for everyone to keep their comments within the two-minute allowed time period. Training team members to report on their ministry in two minutes or less is however very important and beneficial to the organization. Some organizations do something similar every day, normally at the beginning of the day. This keeps everyone informed and up to date with successes, events, breakdowns, and needs.

For instance, my brother works for a large hospital, and one of his first tasks each day is to attend a meeting with all other department heads and upper management. While several gather in one of the hospital meeting rooms, my brother and a few others join the conversation by phone from their offices. Someone in the meeting calls out the name of each department, and the person in charge of that department gives a two-minutes-or-less review of the past twenty-four hours and the needs or activities for the present day. When engineering is called upon, my brother might say, "We will be testing a new generator from 6:00 to 8:00 this evening. So you may see the power flicker as we switch from our regular source to the generator and back." This meeting keeps every team within the organization updated with what is happening within the hospital. Every team leader can then report back to his or her team in a similar fashion. Without this daily meeting, people throughout the hospital would be wondering why the electricity was going on and off that evening, and this could cause panic in a hospital. With this meeting in place, the various departments could prepare for the flickering and the effects on their department, e.g., computers, monitors, life-saving machines, etc.

In the church, a daily ten-to-fifteen-minute meeting could be helpful. However, in many smaller churches, this type of daily meeting may not be conducive. In our story, for instance Marcy serves as a very part-time children's ministry director. She is only at the church one day each week, Tuesday. In any case, a weekly meeting of two-minute reports is essential for properly informed unity of ministry leaders. This can be a stand-alone meeting after everyone arrives for the day, say

9:00 a.m., or it can be included in the regular staff meeting as at 4Cs church in our story.

Decide who needs to be involved, and begin training your staff and key leaders on the two-minute report.

LEADER'S INPUT COMES LAST

Before reading this next section, **Leader's Input Comes Last,** let me give a little insight. The DISC personality type scale has been in use since around 1968. Using assessment tools, people can determine what type personality they generally operate out of. Here is a very brief breakdown: the "D" personality is usually that person driven, assertive, even demanding in some instances. The "D" personality type is what is referred in other circles as an "type-A" personality. "D" type personalities are usually more task oriented than people oriented and want to get the task underway right away.

The "I" personality is that outgoing person who never meets a stranger. "I" personalities can talk to anyone and find starting and carrying conversations a natural part of life. You might have guessed the "I" is more people oriented rather than task oriented.

The "S" personality is also people oriented. One major difference between "S" and "I" personalities is that "S" personalities are more introverted. They are not likely to walk up to a stranger and start a conversation. "S" personalities are reserved and wait for others, though "S" personalities are strong followers.

The last letter in the DISC scale is the "C" personality. These are generally task managers. Detail oriented, "C" personalities are readily busy with the details. They want to make sure all the "i's" have been dotted and every "t" has been crossed before they move forward.

Effective leaders, especially in the church, learn when to speak and when to listen. Working with churches on an on-going basis, I normally meet with the pastor before every meeting with staff or with planning and implementation teams. In the very first meeting with the pastor, I encourage him not to speak first in our conversations and discussions in team meetings, unless I call on him to speak first.

The church is a different organization from most others in several ways. One of those is the respect for the position of leader (pastor). While similar respect is seen in other organizations, in the church more people act out of an "S" personality type than any of the other three (using the DISC personalities descriptor). An "S" personality is people oriented but not the outgoing personality. An "S" personality is not likely to start a conversation with a stranger. This is not comfortable for them. "S" personalities will carry on a conversation with you, but in most cases you need to initiate the conversation.

This behavior plays out in meetings in the church this way: if the pastor speaks first and gives his opinion, most everyone in the room will concede, agree with the pastor, and not make further comment. This is not healthy, as someone else in the room may have a better option for accomplishing the task at hand. Also, it could be that the pastor has not by himself explored all possible avenues. We all act out of our own experience. If the pastor has not been exposed to a particular way of doing something, chances are he may not even think in that realm. Someone on the team, however, may have experienced or read of a different course of action and can bring that into the discussion. It may be that neither the pastor's option nor the member's option is the right one for this church. However, with an open discussion, the team will have a much better opportunity of coming to a healthy outcome and solution that works for this particular congregation.

When the pastor or team leader speaks first, members will resign their thinking to the leader's input. Not only allowing but requesting and encouraging input from each team member leads to healthier outcomes through quality discussion.

MARCY'S HESITATION

Marcy's hesitation is not uncommon. Most people are not risk takers, at least not until they see all the research, hear all the data, and go through everything a second and perhaps a third time. It is not human nature to move forward until a person realizes the risk-versus-reward factor.

Every change, great or small, has a risk-versus-reward factor involved. Simply put, the risk-versus-reward factor demonstrates that the reward to me individually for making this change must be greater than the risk I will expose myself to. For instance, if you are accustomed to having a bowl of cold cereal for breakfast every morning and your doctor recommends a regimen of hot oatmeal every morning, your mind will sift through the benefits of following your doctor's suggestion, weighing them against the emotional attachments to your cold cereal and milk. The emotional attachments to your beliefs and routines of the day are constructed to bring satisfaction and comfort. To change any part of your routine is to stretch you beyond your comfort zone. Marcy's hesitation was not an objection; rather it was an emotional register about her comfort level.

BATHED IN INTENTIONAL PRAYER

In the church we speak of prayer a lot. We know prayer is an imperative to living the Christian life. Yet, in the end we do more talking about prayer than actually praying. I have been in more than one mid-week prayer meeting and other small group prayer times where twenty to thirty minutes were spent on people sharing payer requests for sick friends and family and a few with financial or personal issues. Then after all requests had been rendered, one person prayed for maybe sixty seconds. Do we really enjoy spending more time talking about the ailments of others than praying to our God and Father? It has been said that we spend more time praying to keep sick saints out of heaven than praying lost souls into heaven. In most of these so-called prayer meetings, this is true. Little is said about the lost or our personal quest of obedience to lead others to faith in God.

The average church-goer (regular attendee) spends less than thirty minutes in prayer each week. This includes the prayer times in church, at meals, bedtime, daily devotion, and all other prayer times. Thirty minutes—and that's the best of praying Christians. If you want to see change in your church and in your personal life and ministry, prayer must become a preeminent force. We're not talking about prayer as usual.

As I work with churches, prayer as preeminence comes out very early. As leaders begin to understand and lead their churches in deeper, earnest prayer things begin to happen. God's work begins to shine, and we begin to see signs of rejuvenation. It is not a man thing—it is definitely a God thing. As you consider leading your church in deeper, more earnest prayer, it is okay to study prayer at a deeper level. However, the first thing you must do is go to God in prayer and ask for God's forgiveness for taking prayer so superficially. Then you must ask God to teach you to pray. That may sound "churchy," but not one of us has reached the pinnacle of prayer. I have never heard of or read of a dying saint who said, "I wish I hadn't prayed as much." I have read of some of the greatest prayer warriors and preachers of bygone eras say they would like to have prayed more.

We need to be intentional and intense in our prayer endeavors. We know scripture tells us in James 5:16 that we are to be fervent in our prayers. *"Confess your faults one to another, and pray one for another, that ye may be healed. The effectual fervent prayer of a righteous man availeth much"* (KJV).

Have you ever pondered what fervent prayer means? How far should we take digging in fervently in our prayers? Look at what scripture says about Jesus and fervent prayer. *"Being in anguish, He prayed more fervently, and His sweat became like drops of blood falling to the ground"* (Luke 22:44 HCSB).

Now it's true we only have the one record of Jesus ever praying that fervently—enough to bring sweat drops of blood from His brow. Who among us can say we have prayed so fervently that we have had sweat drops of blood falling to the ground? It is time men and women of God to get intentionally intense and fervent in our prayer life—and not as a one-time event. Will you build it into your DNA?

What could happen if you prayed today, right now, asking God for forgiveness and then asking Him to help you to lead your life and your ministry influence in intentional fervent prayer, bathing every meeting, discussion, and decision in fervent prayer? Throughout this book, you will find the start to several prayers. Study these and learn to go deeper in your prayer life. Why not pause reading and begin now?

Chapter 2

The Interruption

A knock on the door frame of his office brings Pastor Tim out of his study mode. It is Roger: "Sorry to interrupt. It looks like you were pretty deep into whatever you are reading there."

"Yes, I guess I was. It's pretty good reading and eye-opening for me," replies Tim. "What can I do for you on this beautiful first Thursday of June?"

Roger steps through the doorway into Tim's office and asks, "Have you got a minute?"

Tim pushes aside the book he was reading and answers, "Sure, what's up?"

Roger takes a seat and states, "I have a couple of questions," he pauses, before continuing, "I'm having a little trouble with the e-mail you sent to the staff on Tuesday afternoon. I mean the e-mail is all right. But I'm trying to wrap my mind around what exactly you want from us."

"Okay," says Tim turning to his computer, "Let me open up the e-mail and let's look at it together." Tim remembered what he had requested in the e-mail. He also knew it would be better to read it in the context in which it was sent rather than jump right into an explanation. This would help his inquirer, Roger, in discovering the answer to his own question. People learn better when they discover answers for themselves. (**Debrief: Discovery Learning**) He scrolls through his sent messages from earlier in the week. "Tuesday, Tuesday, here it is," announces Tim. He begins to read the e-mail aloud.

"I thank each one of you for your service here at 4Cs and thank you for another good staff meeting this morning. I believe we accomplished what we needed to, and I thoroughly enjoyed our prayer time.

"There is one more thing I want you to consider for next Tuesday's meeting. In moving forward as we discussed this morning, we need a specific focus—one particular point of attention. If we could only focus on one theme or one particular aspect of ministry for the next seven months (till the end of the year), what would that one element be?

"Think on this and bring your idea to our meeting next week. And don't forget to bring your ideas on leading the church in a deeper prayer emphasis."

Looking up from the computer screen, Tim turns back to Roger and says, "That's the e-mail; what's your question? What are you having difficulty with wrapping your mind around?"

"Well," Roger begins, trying to put his query into words. "I'm not sure where you want us to go with this. Is this a test? I mean, we are supposed to be about the Great Commission, right? Then, shouldn't that be our focus?" He pauses for a moment. Tim is silent, but focused on Roger. Without words, the look on Tim's face says, *"Yes, I am listening, I am interested, keep going."* Roger continues, "I also think that since I am the worship minister, I need to be focused on leading in worship. So my answer is worship. Andy is [our] student pastor; shouldn't his focus be on student ministry and discipling those students? The same is true for Marcy and the children's ministry. So, I don't see one particular focus for the whole church, other than the Great Commission."

Tim is still sitting with his head cocked slightly to the side, obviously in a contemplating mode. Ten seconds of silence after Roger finishes laying out his concern seems like two long minutes to Roger. Then Tim begins to speak, "I see you have put some thought into this, and I appreciate your observation and sharing this with me. Let's think through this a little more and maybe I can clarify my desire." (**Debrief:** *Responsive Leading*)

"You are absolutely right. Everything we do should be focused around the Great Commission. And, yes, your responsibility is worship for our congregation, just as Andy's is student ministry and Marcy's pertains to children's ministry." Roger's entire upper body seems to relax with relief at Tim's affirmation of his summation. Tim continues, "And as senior pastor, what is my focus? Preaching, caring for the people, making sure we are a unified team, leading our church to interact with those outside the church. All of these are my responsibility, but which one should be my focus?"

Tim pauses. "You see, we all have multiple areas of focus within our ministries, and we each have separate yet connected ministries." Roger is nodding in agreement, but not sure where this is going, yet.

"Would you agree that we are to be unified?" Tim continues.

"Of course! Absolutely," Roger replies.

"Then, should we not have a unified focus?" queries Tim.

"Well, yes. But I thought that was the Great Commission?" Roger makes a statement but states it in the form of a question to Tim.

"That's good, but is the Great Commission a focus or a directive?" Tim inquires.

As he finishes this question, it appears as a light has turned on in Roger's thinking. And like a little boy receiving a one-dollar bill to go to the candy store, Roger's stature changes. He leans forward in his chair now with a look of renewed joy on his face and says, "Ah, yes, I get it. The Great Commission is our directive—it is what we are supposed to do. Our focus is, 'how are we going to accomplish our directive.' And what you're asking is for us to come up with a unified answer—a focus that covers all of our ministry areas. I've been looking at this all wrong. Thanks, Pastor, now I'll let you get back to your studying, and I'll go work on this for next Tuesday."

Pastor Tim smiles, knowing that Roger has just had a discovery learning experience that he will likely remember a long time—perhaps a lifetime. "You are welcome," he says as Roger walks out the door." With a smile still lingering on his face, Tim pulls the book he had been reading back to the center of his desk and to the center of his attention and study.

Later that afternoon, the intercom on the phone in Tim's office buzzes. It is Susan. "Tim, Greg Bucannon is on the phone for you." Greg Bucannon had worked with Tim as a church health coach at Tim's last church. Tim credits Greg's leadership through coaching as a vital part in helping the church to triple in attendance in seven years. Now, following 4Cs church's vigorous face-to-face summit with reality (an intensive look at the church's true reality), Tim had called on Greg once again for his coaching skills. This was not the first conversation the two men had about 4Cs. Tim reached out to Greg during the process of the vigorous summit and had a follow-up conversation with him discussing the findings of the church's reality. Tim and Roger met with Greg for lunch on the Tuesday following the staff meeting to discuss Greg's role and to firm up expectations for both coach and church.

Tim replies to Susan, "Great! Yes, I've been expecting his phone call." With that comment Tim picks up the phone with a welcome and hearty hello.

After exchanging greetings, Greg takes the lead in the conversation. "I've been reviewing the information you gave me from your vigorous face-to-face summit. The church certainly has an uphill climb, yet it is not quite the situation you found yourself in at Bethany, is it?"

Both men laugh and Tim replies, "No, it isn't!" Following their brief laughter and pause, Tim asks Greg, "So, what do you think?"

"Well, what you are facing, what your face-to-face summit revealed, certainly is not unique to your church. All across our nation, churches are facing similar situations. Fortunately, you and your church have decided to act on it quicker than most churches. The fact that you and apparently your church are willing to try something is a good affirmation to me." Shifting gears, Greg continues, "I'll be there Tuesday for your staff meeting. You can introduce me to the rest of your staff, and we'll go forward from there. Anything else you want me to know today?"

"Yes. About Tuesday; we are going to discuss approaches for leading the church in a prayer emphasis first. I've asked everyone to bring two ideas for leading the church in a prayer emphasis during this turn-around journey," replies Tim. "Then I will turn the meeting over to you and let you begin helping us in finding the one overarching goal. All the staff have been asked to bring one idea for that goal to the meeting. Is there anything else you need from me before Tuesday?"

"Not that I can think of," Greg begins, then hesitates for a second. "Oh yes. Did you talk to the chairman of deacons yet? Is he going to be able to attend the meetings?"

Tim replies, "Yes I have. He is supposed to get back to me today. He's been out of town on business. He was going to check his schedule at work before committing for the rest of the year. He is pretty sure Tuesdays will work for him to be with us."

"Good," replies Greg. "As you remember, he can be a big asset for us in carrying any strategy to the leaders of the church."

Tim is nodding his head as Greg speaks, "Yes, I do remember; to the church, he is one of 'them,' and therefore not only the staff is bringing the strategy to the church. I'm glad you're willing to do this for us, and I'm looking forward to working with you again." (**Debrief:** *Get the Buy-In*)

A quick and brief response from Greg, "Me too, see you Tuesday." And with that the conversation is over.

As Tim hangs up the phone, he begins contemplating what might happen in the next few weeks and months. His mind quickly turns to what could happen if the staff doesn't catch the vision of need in the church. He dismisses that thought, remembering he has been blessed with a good, hard-working, Spirit-led staff. Then his mind turns to the church. What if he and the staff cannot convey the needed changes to the congregation in a manner they will follow? Will he lose his job? He's heard horror stories of pastors being beaten down so much they leave the ministry. Just as quickly as before, Tim realizes what is going on in his head.

This is a spiritual battle. The adversary is trying to distract and discourage him. Tim turns to prayer. Instead of listening to the distractions of the master deceiver, Tim turns to the One who desires to see His church flourish. Tim begins by praying scripture, Psalm 69. Then he continues his prayer praising and thanking God for deliverance from the thoughts and clutches of the evil adversary who would try to throw Tim and his staff off track.

After a time of prayer, Tim pulls a yellow legal pad over and begins writing on it things he knows he must convey to the staff and what the next few weeks of staff meetings might entail. The first item on his list, prayer—deeper, concerted prayer. After fifteen minutes of thinking, prayerfully seeking God's direction, and writing on the legal pad, Tim puts his pen down on the desk beside the pad. He looks at his list, smiles, and says a quiet, "Thank You, Lord. Your ways are the ways I want to tread." With that, Tim begins to gather his things to head home to his wife and children for the evening.

DEBRIEF

DISCOVERY LEARNING

In *Teaching That Bears Fruit,*[2] I wrote about two natural, God-given learning abilities that we each have: discovery learning and imitation. Watching preschoolers who have never been tainted by a formal education system (school or church school), we can observe how they learn. They know no other way but to use their natural, God-given learning abilities. Discovery learning is a great gift from God, and we need to learn to use it in teaching and leading in the church. An example I like to use is an infant crawling around your kitchen following you while you are cooking. You can tell that child fifteen times in five minutes not to touch the stove because it is hot. But when does that child actually learn not to touch the stove because it is hot? You likely just mouthed or at least thought these words, "When he touches the stove."

It is true, the learning takes place with the self-experience, and this is discovery learning. As young adults, we hear our friends stating, "Once you have that first child, your whole life changes." But when do we actually realize what is meant by this statement? When we have our first child, and it is *our* life being radically changed, right? As we grow older, we hear our elders telling of the aches and pains of aging. When do we understand and empathize with what they are saying? When those aches and pains begin occurring in our own lives. These are all acts of discovery learning. The learning is embedded in us as we experience the situation in our lives.

Jesus used discovery learning often in His teaching because He knew that when people discover answers for themselves, they tend to learn better—the learning experience sticks! One such learning experience occurs in the fourteenth chapter of Matthew's gospel account:

Around three in the morning, He came toward them walking on the sea. When the disciples saw Him walking on the sea, they were terrified. "It's a ghost!" they said, and cried out in fear. Immediately Jesus spoke to them. "Have courage! It is I. Don't be

afraid." "Lord, if it's You," Peter answered Him, "command me to come to You on the water."
"Come!" He said. And climbing out of the boat, Peter started walking on the water and came toward Jesus. But when he saw the strength of the wind, he was afraid. And beginning to sink he cried out, "Lord, save me!" Immediately Jesus reached out His hand, caught hold of him, and said to him, "You of little faith, why did you doubt?" When they got into the boat, the wind ceased. Then those in the boat worshiped Him and said, "Truly You are the Son of God!" (Matthew 14:25-33 HCSB).

On this night, I believe Peter had at least two discovery learning experiences. First, stepping over the boat's edge, he discovered he could do something no other man, except Jesus, had ever done—walk on top of water. What an experience—certainly a God-sized, God-oriented experience. The second discovery experience that evening was that he could not continue this miraculous encounter—at least not once he took his eyes and focus off Jesus.

And what about the other disciples—the eleven who remained in the boat grasping the mast in fear of losing their lives in the storm? Did they have a discovery learning experience? The last verse (verse 33) relates they certainly did. *"Then those in the boat worshiped Him and said, 'Truly You are the Son of God!'"*

Discovery learning is a great asset for us as leaders, and we need to learn to employ it. It is not our job as a teacher or leader to always give the answer. It is a greater triumph when we can lead others on a discovery path. Then the learning will be embedded, and we will see lives changed. All of Jesus' teaching and leading was designed to lead His learners in discovery experiences to transform their lives, and it is the directive He has given you and me.

In our story, Pastor Tim could have given Roger a rudimentary answer and ended the conversation quickly—and many leaders would do just that. After all, Roger was an interruption, and interruptions take us away from the important—what we have on our schedule. It is easier to give a quick, to-the-point answer, excuse the interruption, and move on to our schedule. However, this is not always the wisest of decisions. And it is not what Jesus modeled and taught. Jesus almost seemed to welcome distractions. And He used them to offer discovery learning experiences.

What about you? How can you work to implement discovery learning experiences for those you lead or teach? As you continue reading, see how many times Tim uses an opportunity to teach and lead as a discovery learning experience.

For more on discovery learning read chapters two and three of my book, *Teaching That Bears Fruit* (Guardian Books).[3]

RESPONSIVE LEADING

Responsive leading should not be misconstrued as reactive leading. It is not. The two are completely different. Reactive leading is leading after an event or series of events has led to a particular situation. Responsive leading, on the other hand, is leading a subject from the point of his knowledge and understanding to a discovery learning experience.

Notice Tim's response and delivery to Roger's query. Tim did not jump in and begin responding until he knows Roger had sufficiently expounded his inquiry. In fact, when Roger paused, Tim sat quietly yet his facial expression and body language told Roger, "Yes, I am listening, I am interested." When Roger had finished, Tim did not rush into a premeditated answer that he had been plotting while Roger was speaking (contrary to what most of us do). Tim took a few seconds to gather his thoughts. Then, he first recognized Roger's work and showed appreciation for that work. Following this, Tim did not immediately pose a question that might put Roger on the defense. Instead, Tim said, "Let's think through this a little more and maybe I can clarify my desire." Tim placed himself in the boat with Roger. He began his response with "Let's," expressing his desire to walk through this together. Then Tim was ready to assist Roger in a discovery learning experience using a powerful tool of leadership—questions. Also, since Roger was not put on the defensive, he was ready and eager to learn. His mind was not building a defense or meditating on a prescribed answer. Instead, Roger was ready and willing with an open mind to discuss the potential and possibilities of the query at hand.

Notice once again, the questions Tim proposed were formulated to not put Roger on the defensive, but to lead him in discovery—discovering the nature of Tim's e-mail request and discovering a potential common goal or focus for the team to pursue for the rest of the year.

Responsive leading is effective when deployed with the intent of assisting the inquirer in discovery learning. Pacing your response as a leader and formulating the right types of questions is very valuable in the learning process. Will your inquirer learn more from a patient, listening, leader or from one who interrupts, cuts off, and interjects before hearing the full inquiry? Perhaps it is good to practice the golden rule here. You like to be heard and you expect to be heard in full, do you not? Do those subject to your leadership deserve the same respect and hearing?

Practice responsive leading with those subject to your leadership. You'll see greater team effort both in private team meetings and in the public venue where you serve. Responsive leading—listening to the full inquiry without fabricating your response while your subject is speaking. Pause, think through what has been shared, then phrase your response as one with you in the same boat rowing together with your inquirer as a team effort—let's find the solution together.

GET THE BUY-IN

When you want to be successful in a new venture or making a change, it is wise to get those traveling your journey with you to understand and agree with your goal and the plan to reach that goal. This is what I call the buy-in. I have come to the belief that people are not necessarily afraid of change. Fears of change, however, do appear when change appears to be forced on them. In other words, people accept change as it grows on them, as they become comfortable with it.

In implementing change in a church, you will normally find that a small percent (three to five) will grab hold of the vision of the change when you first introduce the idea of change. Some of these are the people you need on your strategy planning and implementation team. As you work through the planning process, a few more will grow comfortable with the idea of the coming change—as long as you keep them informed. Uninformed people are ill-informed people. You do not need to give every detail, but give a steady progression of the planning and implementation strategy. Once you roll out the change, the majority of people will follow along, some with skepticism, others with willing acceptance.

Even after the change has been implemented, there will be yet another three-to-five percent who may be the holdouts. Though they can see the change and perhaps its benefits, these are the unfluctuating few. For some it may appear to be too drastic of a move out of their comfort zone. For others it may be a style or culture change, and for others still it could be a venture away from tradition in the church. Most of these members will in time join the change. While you do not wish anyone to leave your congregation, change will be too great for a few and you may lose them. As a leader you must be ready for this.

You want to minimize this, and the more you can inform the congregation to alleviate their fears and doubts as you move through the planning and implementation phases, the more "buy-in" you will receive from a larger number of members and attendees. As people buy-in to the impending change, they will become agents of change for you. They will also carry the beacon of needed change and adjustment. Providing the change you are making is God centered and Holy Spirit driven, buy-in will be greater and fallout will be lessened. Many pastors and church leaders attempt to implement changes based on their desires and what they have seen or heard of other churches doing. This is dangerous and will cause disruptions and fallout. Not to mention, if it is not God's desired plan of action for the church, it will likely not succeed.

Chapter 3

Tuesday's Meeting

Roger and Marcy are already seated at the table in the meeting room facing the door when Susan walks in at 9:55. Susan takes her place up near the front of the room, near the end of the table where Tim sits. As she places her notebook and calendar on the table, she states, "We're truly all creatures of habit, aren't we? We all sit in the same seats every week."

All three of them chuckle, and Roger replies, "We get here early to get our prize seats so we can see who is coming down the hallway."

Again they all smile and Susan comments, "So that's it. If we move the door, then you two would have to find new seats for a better vantage point." As she finishes her comment, Pastor Tim and another gentleman enter the room.

"Good morning," exclaims Tim to the staff members present. Gesturing to the gentleman with him, Tim begins introductions. "This is Greg Bucannon. Greg, I believe you remember Roger. This is Marcy, our children's ministry director." Turning to his right he holds out an upward turned palm, "and this is Susan, our office administrator who has the full-time task of trying to keep me updated on everything and keeping me straight."

Roger chimes in, "Keeping us all straight and up to date."

Everyone exchanges pleasantries, and Tim motions for Greg to have a seat next to Susan, then proceeds to the end of the table and takes a seat in his normal chair. Focusing his attention back to Greg, Tim states, "There is one more, our youth minister, Andy. He'll be in—"

Roger interrupts, looking at the clock, and says, "—in about two minutes." Susan, Tim and Marcy all smile along with Roger.

Susan places her hand on the table next to Greg as if requesting his attention and says, "You have to know Andy. He is what you might say exactly prompt. If the meeting begins at 10:00, he'll walk in the door exactly at 10:00."

Greg nods and with a smile says, "Well we can't complain about promptness, can we?"

Marcy sparks a little freelance conversation around the table stating, "Coming up with two prayer ideas for the church wasn't so hard. But trying to narrow in on one focus area, that was more difficult. I'm still not sure..." The conversation progresses around the table when the door opens and in walks Andy. Instinctively, everyone—including Greg—looks at the clock on the wall or at their watch.

"10:00," Tim says, "Time to get started." Tim introduces Greg to Andy. Andy takes his seat (the same one he always sits in), and the meeting begins with Marcy sharing a brief four-minute devotion on unity followed by a time of prayer.

Tim thanks Marcy and calls for a change of agenda, stating, "We are going to change things up this morning. We are not going to go through the calendar. Susan will send out by e-mail any changes and additions later today." Everyone seems as if they expect the change and nod in agreement. "Let's begin with our two-minute reports, and Andy, let's begin with you." Andy shares his schedule and pressing ministry needs for the week. The others follow in the same manner, finishing up at 10:15.

"Great. I appreciate each one of you and the ministry you provide," states Tim. "You've all met Greg and know of his work with churches in similar situations as ours. He will be our coach for the next few months as we move through a strategy planning and implementation period in our ministry. Greg will be attending most of our staff meetings and all of our implementation team meetings as well. Roger and I met with Greg last week to catch him up on where we are as a church following our assessment and the reality check, our vigorous face-to-face summit with reality." Everyone turns toward Greg and nods in appreciation. "Greg," Tim continues, "Why don't you share a little about your role with us?"

"Gladly," responds Greg. "My role here is not to give you all the answers or to come up with a plan for your church. Instead, my role as a coach is to help lead you and your team to discover how God has gifted you as a church and what you already have here, in the body, to stop the declining trend and move toward a more healthy, growing congregation of believers. I will do this more by asking you questions than by giving answers. Today, I want to do more observing than coaching. I need to get to know you a little." (Debrief: *Leading by Questions*)

Greg then looks back to Tim, who once again takes the lead in the meeting. "All right. Thanks Greg. Our first assignment was to think of two or three ways that we might be able to lead our church in a prayer emphasis for our 'turn-around journey.' We want to hear everyone's ideas, so let's just start here [gesturing to his right where Marcy is sitting]. Marcy, give us one of your ideas." Marcy looks at her notepad, and almost instinctively, everyone around the table glances at their own notepads as well. (Debrief: *Notepads in the Meeting Room*)

"Well," Marcy responds, "several things came to mind, but I wanted to think of something that could be incorporated not only throughout the church but throughout the entire family. You know, something parents and their children could do together at home. So, I thought we could prepare some sort of devotion or prayer guide and encourage parents…families…to use it at home."

Roger is the first to respond. "I like it. But who's going to write these devotionals?"

Tim interjects, "Let's not get bogged down with the intricacies yet. First let's get all the ideas out on the table. Susan, you write all these down in the meeting notes, and I'll list them on the white board so we can all see them and keep track this morning." Tim turns to write this first option on the board. Verbalizing what he is writing, Tim says slowly, "*Family Prayer Guides*. Good, what else did you have, Marcy?"

"Last week you mentioned training, teaching our people how to pray differently. So I thought we should include that and somehow have training and prayer groups. In other words, invite people to attend specific prayer times and let them know what we want and how to pray for our turn around—the health of the church."

"I had that one listed too." It was Susan interjecting. "We could have different dates and times of the day when people could come to these training groups."

Tim nods his head and begins to write on the board. "Susan, what else do you have, since we know one of yours?" Susan looks at the notes she brought in with her ideas for prayer. "Specific times in each worship service. What if we planned in each worship service a time of prayer specifically for the health of the church and our turn-around journey? Wouldn't that send out a message that we are serious about this and at the same time give an air of expectation to everyone?"

Tim has been writing on the board as Susan was speaking. "I like that and think it is a very good idea. Roger, what about you?"

"Well, I thought about a prayer time in the worship service as well. And I also considered a prayer watch; set aside a specific time frame, twelve hours, or I know churches that have done twenty-four-hour prayer watches where people sign up for prayer times for thirty minutes or an hour to specifically pray for the church—and in this case for our turn-around journey." Again Tim is writing on the board as Roger is speaking. This time he writes *Prayer Watch (12/24 hour)*. Roger continues, "And what about a prayer calendar? We could put out a calendar each month with a particular thing (ministry or person) to pray for each day that relates to our turn-around."

"Okay," says Tim as he writes *Prayer Calendar* on the board.

All eyes turn to Andy, "Andy, I guess that brings us to you. What do you have? Then we'll add any others on your lists," Tim states as he is looking around the room to each of the staff members. Andy leans forward and with exuberance begins, "Since I mainly work with students, I was trying to think what could we do that our students would want to participate in. The one I can see the greatest potential in is small prayer groups that meet on a regular basis. Maybe not forever, but say, six weeks. Then we could start a different emphasis and re-form groups. Groups could meet in homes, not here at the church. It would be more informal, and I believe more people—all age groups—would get involved."

Tim turns to the board and begins writing, *In-Home Prayer Groups (4-6 wks)*. "Okay that certainly has potential, what else?" Tim inquires.

Without hesitation, Andy jumps right back into the conversation, "I thought of several that are on the board, but one that I thought of not listed yet is prayer walks. We could walk the building, parking lot, all of our property. Then we could move out to prayer walk specific neighborhoods and streets. But first, I think we need to start inside our own facilities. If we want God to bless, it has to start here, with us and what we do in here, before we can carry it out to the streets and the people around us."

Having written *Prayer Walks* on the board while Andy was speaking Tim turns to the group and says, "Any others?"

Marcy with a queried look turns to Tim and asks, "What about you? What are your ideas?"

Tim nods, turns his head toward the board and says, "Okay, I thought of prayer in worship services, in-home prayer groups, prayer training groups, all of which are on the board. And I also thought of prayer partners or small accountability prayer groups; two or three people who not only meet to pray together but agree to lift each other up in prayer and check in once or twice a week—encouraging each other to be praying throughout the week for our church."

"Write it on the board," interjects Roger. He then questions, "So now where do we start? They're all good ideas up there and plenty to keep us busy for the next year."

Marcy chimes in with a smile, "The next year and beyond."

Tim nods in agreement, then says, "We don't want to do anything to just 'keep us busy.' The good Lord knows we all have enough to do without more busy-ness, right?" Everyone nods in agreement with smirks and smiles on each face. Tim calls everyone's attention to the eight topics listed on the board.

Family Prayer Guides

Training & Prayer Groups

Specific Times in Worship

Prayer Watch (12/24 hour)

Prayer Calendar

In-Home Prayer Groups (4-6 wks)

Prayer Walks

Prayer Partners

Moving the team to the next step in this prayer planning process, Pastor Tim states, "Now let's look at each one and see what best fits our congregation and where we think God would have us begin."

"*Family Prayer Guides*—how could this be a benefit to our congregation?" Tim turns from the board to glance around the room, allowing team members to submit suggestions before he comments.

"Well," says Andy, "it will give everyone something, a guide, for praying every day for our needs and the ministry of the church."

Susan interjects, "Depending on how they are written, this one could be one of the ways you could teach people how to pray better, deeper, as you were talking about last week. So it could actually cover two areas on our list."

"Good observation," says Tim. "I like that. We could use it as a training tool as well as a daily prayer guide."

Roger drops his pen on his notepad in an intentional attempt for attention, to say, "But I still have the question—who is going to write these? Writing devotions is not such a simple task, and especially if you are going to use them as a training piece as well."

Tim gives one short, quick nod of the head and says, "Roger has a point. Devotions will not write themselves. It takes time, prayer, and Bible study all applied to the theme for the study. And they all need to be alike in format."

"What do you mean 'alike in format'?" questions Marcy. Again, Tim nods and opens his mouth to respond, then seeing an opportunity for learning he changes course. Instead of telling his team what he is speaking about, he decides to lead them on a discovery journey. "Anyone want to take a stab at helping Marcy out? Why would it be imperative to have all the devotions written in like format?"

Another one of those long ten seconds of silence. "Go ahead, someone share with us why you think it is better. Roger, you look like you've got something to say." Roger, head tilted to the right, gazing up to his left in contemplation taps his pen on his notepad three times, stops tapping, hesitates, then shares, "It appears better with a unified look, all written the same way?" What begins as a statement ends more like a question.

"That is true." Tim says. "But there is more than appearance. Why else would it be advantageous for them to be in like format?" Tick, tock, tick, tock, silence again.

Then Andy breaks the silence with a calm and mild-mannered exclamation, "Because it will help create a habit. If they are all written in a particular format, say with questions to answer, scripture to read, and blanks to fill in, that will become part of their study and devotion habits." Andy is speaking with an invigorated confidence because he believes he has discovered the truth to Tim's question. "When we finish this prayer emphasis, their devotion habits will be stronger, and their prayer life will hopefully be deeper!"

As Andy makes his statement of discovery, the body language of Marcy, Roger, and Susan all change as well. Andy and Marcy are sitting taller in their chairs. Roger's furrowed brow gives way to uplifted eyebrows and an air of accomplishment. Tim smiles as he watches the light of discovery once again flash around the table. "Exactly," says Tim with an air of excitement in his voice. "If one day's devotion has good thought-provoking questions, scriptures and blanks to fill in, you do not want the next day to be only a paragraph or two of illustration and a couple of scripture verses."

Susan doesn't give Tim a chance to continue. She adds, "People are creatures of habit and will take the path of least resistance. If you bounce back and forth, they will—at least some of them will—start to skip over the lengthier ones and only read the scripture and pray a little—maybe."

"That's pretty clever," says Marcy. "I never thought of all this when I was thinking of using prayer guides for our church. I was only thinking of something useful for families to use together and individually."

Greg speaks for the first time responding to Marcy's comment. "That's why there are five of you seated around this table. No one has all the answers. When someone, you in this case Marcy, comes up with an idea or option, others in the room can give their input. Together you have the potential to develop a good idea into a great one." (More on Healthy Debate in chapter seven.)

"That's right." Tim chimes in. "We also do not want to forget this one, as Roger has pointed out, will require some extra effort on our part in developing and writing."

Andy jumps into the conversation. "We could all share in that, couldn't we? I know I'm willing to. That way it would not be such a drag on one person's schedule." Roger and Marcy are nodding—though Roger's nod seems more in recognition of what Andy is saying rather than agreeing with him.

Tim responds without hesitation, "We can look at that possibility if we choose to use this one. Anything else on this one?" He pauses for a few short seconds. "Okay then, let's move on to *Training & Prayer Groups*. We know we can use the family devotion guide for part of the training, but what else can we do?" Now that everyone's higher-order thought processes are engaged from the first discovery, the silence has almost vacated the room as they begin to share. The discussion continues for another twenty-five minutes as they think through and discuss each one of the eight ideas listed on the board.

"Well, that's quite a bit," says Tim. "It seems we kind of hovered around four of these. So, which will be our top three to begin working on and praying through? First of all, is there one of these we could implement in the next two to three weeks?"

Andy is quick to jump in and start the conversation. "Yes, the first one might be tough, but pretty much all the others are doable. And since we said we like the top three and in-home prayer groups, I suggest we start there."

Tim inquires of Andy's suggestion, "So, you believe we should focus on training and equipping our people, have a specific prayer time in each worship service, and plan in-home prayer groups?"

All eyes turn to Andy who responds enthusiastically, "Yes, doesn't everyone agree?" There is an air of acceptance in the room, but Tim doesn't sense it is wholehearted buy-in. "Roger, Marcy, what are you thinking? Susan?"

Marcy chimes in first, "Well, it is the four we have been looking at, but I still think the first one, devotionals, will give us—or at least could give us—a stronger foundation for prayer support throughout this process."

Roger tilts his head to the right, then with a slight turn of the head from right to left says, "But it's going to take some work."

Marcy nods in agreement, "I understand. I have written devotions before for parents of our children. I know it is an undertaking. But if we each write one week, just seven devotions, that's a full month." Marcy motions with her pen to Andy, Roger, Tim, and herself. "I'm certainly willing to do my part. I realize it will be an undertaking, but I think we need this part in our prayer emphasis. And besides, like Andy said earlier, it would be part of our training and equipping for our members." Marcy now moves her focus to Pastor Tim. "Pastor, you could tell us how you want them written—what format. It's not like we have to start all three things this week, right?"

Tim nods, but before he can respond, Andy jumps in. "Absolutely, we can start with the prayer time in the service and explain to the congregation that this is the first element of a prayer emphasis we will be rolling out over the next few months. And it will be training for our people. Many of them need to be instructed how to pray." Andy has everyone's attention. They understand what Andy means by his last statement. Nonetheless he offers the following explanation. "We all know that many in our church have particular prayer habits, praying certain ways, using the same statements and requests over and over. What we're talking about is deeper prayer, a more personal, yet deep-rooted and profound time with God, right?" Andy pauses again as he looks for affirmation from the others.

Marcy and Tim are looking directly at Andy, Roger's eyes are on the notepad in front of him, Susan is copiously taking notes, but it is clear everyone is in agreement with Andy. He continues, "I think Marcy is right on every count as to why we should work on this. It may be September before we roll it out, but we need to begin working on it now."

Everyone is quiet, taking in everything Andy and Marcy have shared. Tim allows about a ten-second silence before he is ready to respond. "I believe you two have given a valid reason for including this in our plans. And since I do not hear anyone else, can I assume we are all in agreement and willing to move forward?" Tim glances around the room then stops his focus on Greg, knowing he has something to say. "Greg, it looks like you have some input here. What is it?"

Greg leans forward in his chair, ensuring everyone can see him. "You two [looking at Andy then quickly to Marcy] make some very good points for this. And they are points hard to argue against." Leaning forward to look beyond Susan and to look Andy in the eye, Greg continues, "And it is not just your church. Many churches have people in them with kind of a stale prayer life and style. I recently heard a college student when called upon to bless a particular meal said, 'God is great, God is good. Thank you for this food. Amen.' This was a college student—who has been in church all his life. We apparently have not done a very good job at equipping our people in praying the way the Bible teaches. When called upon, many people in our churches have a fear of praying in public. And they admit they do not know how. At least this young man did not hesitate. He prayed what he knew. That is apparently all he had ever been taught. We need to do a better job, and I think you are on a good and right track going into writing these devotions with this in mind. Teach them to pray."

Tim picks up right where Greg stops. "The disciples did not ask Jesus to teach them to preach or teach or even heal. But they did specifically ask Him to teach them to pray. And in His response, Jesus did not say pray this and gave them the words to say. Rather He said when you pray, pray like this."

Roger takes the opportunity to use some of his seminary learning to say, "That's why it is referred to in theological realms as the model prayer."

Tim nods and says, "Okay, that one will take some time, and I will work on a 'model' [playing off Roger's comment] devotion for us. I also can think of two or three people in our congregation who could help us write the prayer devotions. It does not have to all come from this room. After all, we are to lead our people, right? So, what else can we begin right away?"

"Inserting a special prayer time in the worship service is pretty easy." Roger has joined the conversation and nods toward Tim as he continues, "That pretty much is reliant on you and me, Pastor. We can work on what that should like and where to place it in the service." Within five minutes, the team has agreed upon a plan to begin a special prayer time in the worship service immediately and to begin working on training and equipping the church for a special emphasis on prayer. Assignments have been made, and the team is ready to move on.

Tim gives a statement of encouragement and thanks the team for their input then states, "Next, we need to talk about your ideas for our overarching goal or theme for the next seven months—till the end of the year. Who will go first?"

DEBRIEF

LEADING BY QUESTIONS

One of the greatest God-given tools any leader has is the question. It is like a multi-purpose tool and can be used in a variety of ways for differing results. With a question, you can seek knowledge and information. Questions can also be used to determine the knowledge base and experience of your listeners as well as their understanding of the topic. Attorneys and other leaders use questions to ascertain truth. Questions are a great tool to influence discovery learning. And as we have seen in our story, questions can be used to stimulate higher-order thought processes.

Learning to lead by using questions, in my opinion, brings a thrill and joy to leadership. However, it is a learning process. I've been in too many situations where a leader or teacher could have had great production and a learning experience had he or she used a better question. For some reason, in churches we are prone to use the type of question that produces the least amount of learning. In fact, it very seldom produces learning at all. It is the closed-ended question. Closed-ended questions normally have one specific and often brief answer. The main reason closed-ended questions produce little or no learning is they rely only on static recall. The following is an example of a closed-ended question: What day of the week is today?

In many of our churches today there is a standing joke that says, "If the teacher calls on you to answer a question, just answer Yes, No, or Jesus and you'll be right." We have trained our people not to think. We must learn to use questions and leadership methods like those Jesus used to transform lives and ministry effectiveness. When we use closed-ended questions, we do not allow our listeners to use their higher-order thought processes. Therefore true life-changing learning cannot take place, and effective ministry is squandered in meetings instead of in the marketplace.

As leaders, the more we can learn to use properly formulated questions, the greater our leadership will be practiced and followed. Instead of closed-ended questions, we need to learn to use open-ended questions. There are many forms of open-ended questions. All open-ended questions lead to higher-order thinking and produce results and learning. Remember the closed-ended question above, "What day of the week is today?" The very second someone calls out the answer everyone's thinking shuts down; everyone in the room stops thinking.

Instead of that particular closed-ended question why not ask this question, "What does Saturday mean to you?" Do you see the difference? Instead of one specific and brief answer, everyone in the room begins contemplating what is meaningful to him or her about Saturday. And when one person answers, the thinking of others does not shut off. Instead, everyone takes what was shared and compares it to his or her own thoughts. Some will add to, others will take away from their thinking of what Saturday means. If five or six people respond, or twenty, everyone in the room continues in the higher-order thought processes, comparing, adding to, subtracting, and contemplating until you, the leader, says it is time to move on.

In leadership, this type of question can be invaluable in strategic planning and implementation of effective ministry and growing disciples. The more you can study and learn to use questions—properly formulated questions—the more effective your leadership and the ministry of your organization will be. For more on leadership by questions, read *The Art of The Question*, chapter four of *Teaching that Bears Fruit*, or read Formulating Questions at soncare.net.[4]

NOTEPADS IN THE MEETING ROOM

One thing you might notice in the story, everyone uses a legal pad to take notes in meetings. Pastor Tim does not allow computer usage during planning meetings—something he learned from coach Greg Bucannon. I realize this is like a cold, hard wind in the face for modern technology and "techies" who have become accustomed to using computers, electronic tablets, and pads in meetings today. Be sure to read this section to the end before dismissing this idea. I like to use them myself; however, I have witnessed firsthand the distractions caused in meetings and believe they should be left powered down in planning meetings. Likewise, in our story, Tim is of the belief that computers are a distraction in meetings. If one person is on a computer, it can cause distractions to everyone in the room. The constant sound of keys being pecked will distract from the deeper-level thinking processes. Some might say many of today's keyboards are nearly silent when in use. However the movement of hands and typing motion send the same distraction to others seated around the computer user, not to mention the user is not interacting with people but with a computer screen.

Also, the leader and other participants find themselves wondering what the man or woman with the computer is working on. Are they really engaged in the meeting? Is he checking e-mail, social media, or box scores? A computer user will bring distractions like this to others in the room. Another distraction; while typing, the computer user loses contact with full engagement of the discussion at hand. Some would say, "Not me. I can do both." Yet in various studies in North America and Europe, multi-tasking has been disproven. As much as we like to think we can fully engage in two things at once, the brain is incapable of such a feat.

Not only the cognitive distractions for the computer user and other participants, there is also physical distraction involved with computer usage. In any meeting, a computer user, even if he or she is simply using it to take notes, will likely keep visual contact with the monitor, therefore losing focal contact with the others in the room and in the discussion. Since a person's words make up only seven percent of our total communication, eye contact and body language are vitally important from everyone on the team for full engagement in a group discussion. It is my observation that a person using a computer cannot remain in full engagement with the discussion than others.

There is an exception that has been brought to my attention: tablets with handwriting recognition. There are some electronic tablet-type devices that work exactly as a pen and paper legal pad. These devices allow the user to handwrite notes on the screen with a stylus or finger that get automatically translated into note-taking software on his or her computer.

I realize the day is fast approaching when electronic tablets and notepads will overtake other means of note-taking in meetings. My intent here is to communicate a very real distraction in meetings that will keep you from fully engaging everyone in the room in the discussion. Patrick Lencioni also wrote about this in his book *Death by Meeting*.

For the record, there is usually at least one computer in the room at Tim's meetings. But it is there for reference only. If the team needs to look something up to assist in the progression of the meeting, the computer is used at that time. Implement this in your planning meetings, and engagement will improve and greater discussion can be yours as a team.

Chapter 4

Overarching Objective

Immediately as Tim finishes his question "Who will go first?" it is Andy who jump starts the conversation; remember, he's the young, energetic, ready to take on the world, student minister. "I believe we should focus on reaching new people. If we focus on getting new people in here, will that not stop the decline? We'll be adding, not subtracting."

"Okay, I'll write that one on the board," says Tim.

"I don't know," Roger chimes in, remembering his conversation in Tim's office the previous Thursday. "That's only one part of the Great Commission, our purpose. And besides, the Great Commission is our directive and not necessarily our focus."

With a perplexed look, Marcy jumps in, "Wait, what do you mean not our focus? We've agreed that everything we do should focus on the Great Commission."

Roger looks a little embarrassed, then replies, "I'm sorry. Maybe I didn't say that right. Tim did a better job explaining it to me last week." Turning to look at Tim, Roger continues, "Perhaps you should clear up my mess here. You know what I'm trying to say."

With a slight shake of his head right to left and then back again, Tim responds, "No. You try it again. You are close. What is the right wording to get it out?" (Debrief: *Reinforcement of Discovery Learning*)

"Well, let's see." Roger is hesitating, gathering his thoughts. He looks down at his paper. There is nothing written on it. He is trying to remember how Tim said it to make it so instantly clear to him on Thursday. After a moment, he is ready to continue. "I was struggling with this last week and went to see Tim in his office. I first said the Great Commission is to be our focus, just like Marcy. Then Tim asked me a question. 'Is the Great Commission a focus or a directive?' It immediately hit me. I was looking at this all wrong. The Great Commission is our directive—what we are supposed to do! Our focus is how we are going to accomplish that directive. It must be something that can cross all ministry lines so we can all—as a church—embrace it." He pauses for a few seconds then adds, "So actually Andy's suggestion could be a potential focus or overarching theme."

Tim is standing with a slight smile on his face as Thursday's student, Roger, has now become the teacher due to his discovery learning experience in Tim's office. "Would you mind expounding on that? I mean, why do you say now that this could be our overarching theme when just minutes ago you were ready to challenge it. What changed your mind?" Tim wasn't trying to embarrass Roger for changing his mind. Rather, Tim wanted Roger and the others to see and understand what caused the change. This is reinforcing the discovery learning experience.

"Well—" the thought wheels are turning before Roger offers his explanation. "If we plan it right, bringing new people in is the first step. We cannot teach them if we do not bring them in. So reaching new people could be part of our overarching theme. But it still seems a little vague. Do you know what I mean?" Roger finishes his explanation, looking around the room, desiring affirmation and input from everyone.

Tim scans the room. Everyone is pondering what Roger has said. "Okay, do we want to flesh this one out more right now or get everyone's thoughts?" With a very short pause Tim continues, "Why not get everyone's ideas on the board first. Then we can discuss them and give our input. Susan, how about you? What did you bring to the table for our overarching theme?"

Looking up from taking notes for the meeting, Susan shifts in her chair as if shifting from clerk to speaker mode and says, "I believe unity is what we need. Unity will bring us together as a church to rally around our focus today and for years to come."

"Okay," says Tim as he turns to write *Unity* on the board for all to see just under reaching new people. "Marcy?" Tim questions as he finishes the last letter, and with his back still turned to the table. "What is your thought for our theme?"

"I thought a lot about this, trying to take the overall church perspective. I thought about unity and evangelism—reaching people. I also thought about communication. We could certainly improve on that around here." Then, almost seeming surprised at her own words, Marcy quickly adds, "Oh, not that we're bad, but there's always room for improvement, you know?"

Roger lets out a small, quiet laugh and the others all smile at Marcy's clarification. Tim inquires, "Is that your submission—communication?"

"Oh, no!" Marcy jumps back in. "I guess I didn't communicate that well." Everyone laughs at Marcy's comedic interjection on communication. She continues, "I believe our overarching goal should be on families. With summer upon us, families take vacations together and attend cookouts and other outings. In the fall, families rally around back to school and getting back into the groove of things. And then there are the holidays. Thanksgiving and Christmas are celebrated with family. It will give us a great opportunity—" with a stronger emphasis, Marcy continues—"an ongoing opportunity, to reach people and unify the church around our theme that already involves ninety percent of our members."

"You certainly have thought through a lot, haven't you? Little Miss Detail," Roger comments with a serious yet lightweight affirmation of Marcy's idea.

Tim, who had turned with an intrigued interest in Marcy's oration, now turns back to the board and writes *Family*. "Roger," he says while still writing, "That leaves you. What have you come up with?"

"I believe spiritual growth or spiritual depth would be a good focus for us. However you want to say it: growth or depth."

"Okay, great," says Tim. "Four good ones. All four have potential. Now—"

Before Tim can finish his statement, Roger jumps in: "Wait, what about you? Aren't you going to give us one?"

"No," states Tim. "I do not want to taint your thinking. So we're going to choose one from these four."

Marcy quips, "But, what if you have a better one?"

Tim purses his lips and gives a very slight shake of the head as he says, "I don't. These are good. I couldn't come up with a better one. Let's look at these one by one." Tim puts down the marker he's been writing with, turns to Greg and says, "Greg, why don't you lead us through this next discussion in finding our overarching theme?" Tim offers his statement as a question, but it is obvious he is relinquishing his role as leader to Greg to coach the team through this discussion. (**Debrief:** *Using a Coach from Outside the Organization*)

"Alright, I think I can handle that," quips Greg. Remaining in his seat and turning to face the white board for a quick look at the topics, he says, "Okay, let's start with the second one, unity. Susan, I believe this was your suggestion, correct?"

Still taking notes, Susan does not look up from her pad and answers, "Yes."

Greg indulges, "Anything else you want to say about why you chose unity?"

Laying her pen down on her pad, Susan begins: "It's not that unity doesn't exist around here, but there is always room for improvement. And I believe the more we can work on and improve the unity of the church, the better we'll be at growing the church. We'll be—unified. I sit out front in the office, and I am usually the first person people see and the one to answer the phone most often when they call. So I see and hear more than most of the staff." It is as if Susan is talking directly to Greg, who is sitting to her right. Glancing back around the room, she continues, "We've talked about this before." She's looking for affirmation from the others. The other four staff members all nod in agreement. "It's like people don't listen or read their program; they never visit the website." Directing her comments back to Greg, "We do not have a major problem. It's just...maybe Marcy's idea of communication and unity should go together. Do you know what I mean?" Her last question was definitely addressing everyone in the room.

Andy leans forward with his head and shoulders over the table, "Yes. I do. And I think we all understand what you mean, and we could certainly do a better job. As you said earlier, 'There is always room for improvement.' I'm just not sure that is our overarching theme we need to be addressing right now. It can certainly be addressed through some of these others."

"You're never going to get everyone on board." It's Roger. "I mean some people are just never going to—" Roger stops in mid-sentence, then continues, "Let's face it, church unity is an oxymoron." He laughs as he finishes the statement, and everyone enjoys a brief moment of laughter with him.

Greg takes the opportunity to interject, "Andy, tell me a little more about what you mean when you say, 'It can be addressed through some of the other ideas on the board.'"

"If we're working on families as our overarching theme, are we not taking a unified body of four or five people and working to unify seventy-five of these family units as one? And spiritual growth is all about unity in my mind. How can you have spiritual growth as a church and not have unity? My idea of reaching out includes a unified effort of reaching the community around us with the Good News. I think unity is included in all of the above."

Marcy jumps in, "Isn't that the whole purpose of this exercise?" She hesitates briefly. "Isn't the purpose of an overarching theme to unify or bring unity throughout the church?" Marcy turns toward Tim, leading everyone in the room to do the same. Tim is smiling. "What?" queries Marcy. "What are you smiling about?"

Tim tips his head to the left and says, "I think that is a great observation. I think you hit the nail on the head. Whatever our overarching theme is, I think it needs to produce unity. Andy was saying it without realizing it. You realized it and brought it to the forefront. That's what we want."

Greg takes the lead again. "Okay, anything else on unity for now?" After a brief pause, Greg continues, "If not, then let's move on to families. Why would families be a good overarching theme?"

Roger begins the dialogue: "Marcy gave us a good reason with the reminders of what families are already involved in for the next seven months: vacations, school, sports, holidays. I think that is a good why, and I also believe it is a ready-built unit. It is people of common ground and interests. Pique their interests, and they will work together with other families; especially families of like age and life stages."

"I agree," contributes Andy. "Families are natural starting blocks for us. And there are many angles where we could use the family element in fulfilling the Great Commission—our purpose during this period and this overarching theme. Block parties, families reaching families—"

Roger jumps in, "Doing mission projects together locally."

Marcy, who has been eagerly and excitedly listening to some of the same things she had considered before coming into the meeting, now takes her opportunity to interject. "Exactly, families praying with each other and for one another, helping with project back to school, and school needs, community needs during the holidays, food baskets, Christmas for the needy. There's so much."

Roger reaches over and places his hand on the table in front of Marcy as if to quiet an excited child. "Whoa there, girl. Calm down. Don't get too excited yet." Everyone enjoys a quick laugh. "I can see this is more of that deep thought you put into this."

Marcy can't help but smile, "Yes it is. There is so much we can do. Families can give testimonies. We could have family retreats and special Bible studies."

Tim looks at Greg and states so everyone can hear, "Once you get her started, it's hard to stop her."

Everyone laughs again and with a smile still on his face, Greg says, "Well, the question was 'why' and quickly turned to 'how,' which is okay. That was going to be my next question. Let me ask you another question. What is another advantage for using families as our overarching theme?"

Susan, who has been silently taking notes during the discussion, looks up from her notes and says, "Most of our families are already connected to others in their age bracket in Sunday school. It should be a natural motivator to get involved together with other families for those types of events and projects."

"Exactly," exclaims Greg with excitement in his voice as he looks around the room to garner excitement from everyone else. "What else might that do for you?"

Tim, who has tried not to interject too much in the conversation, speaks up: "Well, it could help us get some of those sideline Christians, our fringe people involved." The staff knew what Tim was talking about. He has used the term *fringe people* before. Tim is referring to those members and regular (or semi-regular) attendees who attend service but never get involved. "I believe a large part of them will get involved in something if we take the time and effort to involve them."

Greg is nodding in approval. "That's good. Very good. I like all of this, and it sounds like perhaps you all have hit on something. But before we go any farther, with families, we've got one more: spiritual growth. Let's discuss that one. Roger, get us started. I believe this was your submission."

"Are you kidding?" Roger begins while flipping his pen out of his hand and onto his notepad. "I concede to families." Again everyone enjoys a quick laugh. "There's no need to discuss this one, let's add it to families and get started."

Everyone still smiling, Andy tips his head to the right and says, "He's got a point." Looking directly at Roger, he continues, "I don't know if you're serious or not, but what better opportunity can we have for reaching others and to produce spiritual growth than through the family? I believe it is the best way we can reach more people in the next seven months, so mine is included in families as well."

Looking at the others in the room then stopping at Greg, Roger raises the question, "What do you think?"

Greg looks at Tim then turns his glance to Marcy, Susan, then to Andy. "I'm here to facilitate and coach you through this. You tell me."

Tim quietly scans the room, reading everyone's body language. After a moment of silence, Marcy speaks up, looking directly at Roger, who is seated to her right. "Are you sure? There is plenty that could be said for spiritual growth and depth in our church."

Roger begins to nod when Greg interjects: "That's good, Marcy. Give us one of those reasons for choosing spiritual growth." Greg is pretty sure the group has reached a consensus, but as a church health and life coach he also knows it will be best to let everyone share their ideas. Doing so will ensure all ideas are on the table, and it can all be used to solidify the team's position. For the next four to five minutes, Greg guides the discussion around the table about deeper spiritual growth as an overarching theme. At the end of the discussion, a decision is made. The decision is unanimous on the overarching theme.

Pastor Tim straightens up in his chair, leans into the table, and with a look of satisfied accomplishment on his face says, "Thanks. This is why I think we make a good team. We have spent most of the last two hours trying to unearth and discover two very important things for the future of this church. You work as a team—we worked as a team and got it done. You are all gifted, and I appreciate you and what you bring to the table and do in service for God and our church. This is a great start, but it is only the beginning. God has great things in store, and you are the team that can carry it out. Let's go get some lunch and commit to pray for these decisions and the implementation of things to come." (**Debrief:** *Sending with Affirmation, Follow Up, and Accountability*)

DEBRIEF

REINFORCEMENT OF DISCOVERY LEARNING

Tim wasn't trying to embarrass Roger for changing his mind. Rather, Tim wanted Roger and the others to see and understand what caused the change. This is reinforcing the discovery learning.

We have often heard that repetition produces learning. I cringe a little when I hear this because I am not certain repetition by itself can create a learning experience. In our story, Tim asked Roger to explain the meaning to assist Roger in a clear and better understanding of what Roger had learned in Tim's office. It is why our elementary school teachers had us come to the front of the class and solve math problems. What seemed difficult (and scary) to us then, we now consider simple, easy math. It wasn't necessarily the repetition, but working it out in our mind, having the "how" picture painted mentally over and over.

When we allow people to take their discovery learning experience and put it into practice and verbalize it for others, the new wisdom and knowledge becomes embedded and ingrained in his or her mind, locking it into our long-term memory. As you ascertain the use of discovery learning, be certain to take advantage of opportunities to provide reinforcement of discovery learning as Pastor Tim did with Roger. Watch for Tim to use this leadership trait with others as you continue reading.

USING A COACH FROM OUTSIDE THE ORGANIZATION

In *Reaching the Summit: Avoiding and Reversing Decline in the Church*,[5] I gave account of why I believe if you want to turn your church around, you need the assistance of someone from the outside: a well-trained, experienced coach. A coach is one who sees your ministry from a totally different perspective from anyone in your organization. Everyone inside the church, including the pastor, has a biased viewpoint. It is natural and cannot be avoided. Seeing from this outside vantage point, a trained and experienced coach can then formulate good thought-provoking questions—questions that church leaders and members may not think of or may be afraid to ask.

I have had people ask, "Why can't we do this on our own, without a coach from outside the church?" This may at first sound like a reasonable question. However, think about it, who has been helping you on your ministry journey thus far? It is the same people that you are implying can help you make the turn-around. The simple response to the question, "Why can't we do this on our own?" is "How has that been working for you so far?" The people inside your church are generally not bad people, but the perspective they have has not led you to turn around or make needed changes in recent history. You need the objective eye of an outside observer, one experienced in assisting churches in this manner.

The well-trained, experienced coach I am speaking of is someone who has helped lead churches through this type of turn around and who is trained and experienced in formulating good thought-provoking questions; one who can help the church to discover and unearth the hidden qualities and strengths within the church. The coach then leads the church in developing and implementing those strengths using biblically based principles to fulfill God's purpose for the church.

A coach is someone who is not wanting to come in and give you all the answers and suggestions. Rather, a truly good coach will guide you in discovering what God has already made attainable within your church. What gifts, talents, strengths, and other resources do you have sitting in your church that have not been put into practice or have not been utilized to their greatest potential? I believe every church has what it needs to begin the turn-around process. In many cases, it is simply a matter of unearthing and developing those gifts, strengths, and resources.

Do not get caught up in the "We've got to do it like First Successful Church across town" comparison. That is copying models. Let an experienced coach guide you in discovering and developing the principle-based strengths God has already placed within your reach. For more information on selecting a coach that is right for your church, visit www.soncare.net or contact SonC.A.R.E. Ministries.

SENDING WITH AFFIRMATION, FOLLOW UP, AND ACCOUNTABILITY

Tim begins his closing remarks in the meeting with an affirmation of everyone involved. People need and desire affirmation. While our goal is not to acquire the affirmation of others, we have an imbedded need to receive affirmation for our labors and efforts.

Many meetings in church and business end without any commitment to follow up or accountability. Without commitment to follow up, the likelihood of accomplishment diminishes dramatically. In a meeting, when a decision is made, assignments for undertaking the task should also be made. When assignments are made or challenges issued, if follow up does not occur, accountability wanes. A good leader instills the need for assignments to be made, and a course of accountability is set. We'll talk more about accountability later.

In our story, no action decisions were made. Therefore, one may not see a need for follow up and accountability. Notice, however, how Pastor Tim closes the meeting: "Let's go get some lunch and commit to pray for these decisions and the implementation of things to come." Does he build in follow up and accountability? Certainly. "Let's go get some lunch and *commit to pray…*" With three words, he gave the assigned follow up and accountability. The assignment was not only to pray, but to *commit* to pray. And the one word *commit* also depicts accountability.

Regardless of what your team, staff, or committee is contemplating, if there is no follow up and accountability taking place, is there really any forward progress taking place? Even in what seem to be routine meetings (preparing a budget, reviewing the church calendar, discussing present or future ministries), you are only setting the course for tomorrow when you build in follow up and accountability. Like preaching or teaching without issuing a challenge, are you not in effect only dispensing knowledge? Dispensing knowledge does not cause learning or growth. Though it might produce trivia buffs.

Practice building in follow up and accountability in all your meetings and ministry. Jesus did; follow up and accountability were active parts of each meeting, lesson, and teaching session with His disciples.

Chapter 5

The Luncheon

The team arrives at the restaurant in two separate vehicles, and walking across the parking lot, there seems to be at least two conversations going on between the six men and women. The spontaneous conversations continue as they are seated, and a waitress comes to take everyone's drink orders. The casual conversations are ongoing when the waitress returns with drinks and begins taking everyone's food orders. She asks for Greg's order last, and Greg takes the opportunity to engage the waitress in conversation. "Jenn—you said your name was Jenn, right?"

"Yes," she replied.

"Jenn, can I ask you a couple of questions to help us out with a project we are undertaking?"

Jenn replies, "Certainly. What can I help you with?"

"Our project has to do with families in this area, this community. Do you mind if I ask who your immediate family consists of? I mean do you live with family?"

Jenn gives a couple quick nods and says, "Yes I do. My husband and I have a three-year-old daughter."

Marcy, Roger, and Susan all in one accord let out an "Ahh!" with the thought of a three-year-old girl in the house.

Greg continues, "Great, thank you, Jenn. What would you say is the biggest need for young families like yours in our community?"

Jenn tilts her head to the left and says, "My, that's a tougher one. I might have to think on that one."

Greg, not wanting to lose the momentum, jumps in quickly: "Okay, tell me what is the one thing you and your husband could use more of—other than money?" Greg finishes with a laugh.

Jenn thinks for a second, then says, "Time," giving a slight yet quick nod. "More time with each other. My husband works third shift, and I work here during the lunch and afternoon hours. He watches our baby while I'm at work, and I am home with the baby so he can rest in the evening and while he works overnight. So we really could use some more time together as a family—and as a couple."

Greg, with a grateful smile, says, "Thanks Jenn. That is very helpful. There is one more question, then I'll let you go. We are going to pray before our food gets here, and we would like to pray for you. We will pray that God gives you and your husband some quality time and family time too. Is there anything else we can pray about for you?"

Jenn responds with a grateful smile of her own. "No, I don't think so. That will be plenty if you could pray for time."

As the waitress walks away from the table, Greg looks around and notices differing facial expressions on the staff members. Some have a look of embarrassment that they did not think to ask the waitress how they could pray for her. Others sat with a look of wonder and surprise at the exchange that had just taken place. Marcy is the first to speak. Looking directly at Greg, she states, "That was just short of amazing. You engaged her in a brief conversation and got an outside perspective on what we want to accomplish."

Greg nods three times, each one slightly smaller than the one before and remarks, "It's that simple and easy."

Roger jumps in, "But first you asked for her permission."

Greg nods again, twice this time. "And that is important. When we ask for people's permission, they almost always grant it. We simply don't think to ask often enough. And one other thing about the way I asked those questions. Nobody likes to be told, but everyone loves to give their opinion. When you ask the proper questions, you are asking for another person's opinion. People love to give their opinion. So why not ask good questions?"

A couple of separate and casual conversations break out around the table. As the conversations settle down, Susan looks across the table and asks Greg a question. Tim, who is sitting next to Greg, hears the question and interrupts, asking Greg to wait before answering. Tim, calling for everyone's attention says, "I would like for everyone to hear this. Susan has asked Greg a great question that we all need to hear. Susan, would you ask your question again so everyone can hear?"

Susan, with a little bit of surprise, gladly accepts Tim's request. "Yes. What I asked was, 'We've settled on families as our overarching theme and had some discussion about it; what do you see as our next steps?'"

Greg, clearing his throat, begins: "Well, as Pastor Tim stated back at the church, what you accomplished today is good. But it is only the beginning. If you go out and try to implement what you spoke of today, it will not go well. Oh, you might do some good, but you will have missed the greatest of opportunities." Greg pauses, looking around the table as if inviting the next question. Actually, he is allowing time for his comments to sink in, knowing the pause will engage the higher-order thought processes of each of his listeners. (**Debrief:** *Engaging Higher-Order Thought Processes*)

Marcy is the first to respond, "What do you mean? What opportunities would we miss?"

Nodding his head, Greg replies, "Good question, and one I anticipated. Coming up with good or even great ideas does not guarantee success. Think of it this way. If you are planning a trip, there are a few things you want to know. What is the first vital piece of information you need before you can plan or take a trip?" Silence pervades for a long seven seconds.

Then Roger jumps in, "Where you are going. You need to know where you are going before you can plan or go on your trip."

As if Roger just gave the correct answer for Final Jeopardy, Greg enthusiastically says, "Yes, exactly. You cannot take off until you know your destination and what direction. What might be the next important piece of information?"

This time Andy is ready with an answer: "How will you travel, car, boat, airplane?"

Greg looks down the table to Andy, though he continues to address everyone. "Okay, that's good. Now let's say you are driving and you are on your trip. How will you know you are making progress?"

Andy again is ready with an answer. "The mile markers. You know by the mile markers and highway signs. If you start off with a seventy-five mile drive and you see a sign that says your destination is only thirty-three miles away, you know you are making progress."

"That's right again, Andy. Good job." Greg approves of Andy's analogy. "I like to call these the destination indicators. Destination indicators are like mile markers, highway signs, and points of interest along the journey."

With an expression of confusion on her face, Marcy looks across the table at Greg and joins the conversation. "Okay, I get the analogy with cars and driving. But how does that have anything to do with our overarching umbrella of reaching and ministering to families?"

Focusing his eyes on Marcy's, Greg nods with a gaze of kindheartedness for her understanding. Then he turns to the others around the table and queries, "Does anyone want to take a shot at it before I comment?" (Debrief: *Probing the Learning and Understanding*)

Roger rejoins the conversation. "Well, I guess it is not only good to know what you hope to accomplish—to drive seventy-five miles east. You also need to know along the way that you are making progress. In other words, we need some mile markers in our plan. Things that will show us we are making progress, reaching families as we go. Otherwise we will be spinning our wheels, maybe driving somewhere, but not really sure if we are moving toward our destination. I'm not sure what our mile markers would be for reaching and ministering to families but—"

Greg interrupts Roger, "That's okay, because that is one of the next steps that Susan was asking about. You see, Marcy, you can find several ways to reach out to families and minister to families, just like you can choose several ways to get to your destination. But how will you know you are making good, viable progress?" Greg now looks around the table, making certain to catch everyone's eyes with his, then continues, "Just doing events or ministry efforts does not guarantee success or even forward progress."

Everyone nods in agreement, and Roger throws in an amen, while Andy states, "Boy, don't we know that one."

Marcy's expression hasn't changed much as she asks, "So, how do we do that? Are we supposed to come up with a set of numbers—how many families we want to reach? How many new families we want to have in our church by the end of the year?"

Greg's gaze is fixed on Marcy again, "Not necessarily. You could use numbers as part of your determining indicators, but we'll need to spend some time thinking through these and coming up with really viable and achievable ones for your overarching goal—your destination." Looking back to the others around the table Greg continues, "And destination indicators are only one of the next steps to investigate."

Marcy, says, "What? You mean there's more?"

"Sure," Greg answers, "When you are driving your car, you watch not only the road in front of you, what else do you watch?"

Roger, with a smile says, "Well, if you're Andy, you watch everything around you, everything except the road." Everyone enjoys a chuckle. Roger continues, "No, seriously, you watch your gauges. You watch your speedometer, your gas gauge, your temperature gauge. And you're watching your mirrors."

Greg is nodding. "Right. You need driving gauges in your quest to reach your overarching goal as well. What are those things you can see at a glance to give you an appraisal of your situation—no matter where you are on your journey? Your gas gauge tells you how much gas you have at the moment, right?" Nods come from around the table. "Your gas gauge does not tell you how much gas you had a half hour ago or when you left home. It is a current statistic, isn't it?" Greg is scanning the faces of the other five to make certain they understand. "So we need to look at destination indicators and driving gauges."

Tim, who has played the quiet listening leader thus far, interjects. "This sounds like it will take more than a two-hour meeting?" It is a statement, but Tim forms it into a question for Greg and quickly asks a follow-up question to go along with it. "Should we set aside some time for a staff retreat to work on these?"

Greg is nodding before Tim finishes his question, then responds, "Yes, that would be great if you could. As you know," he's looking at Tim, "from past retreats with me, discussions like this are sometimes hard to place a time limit on."

Tim has another question, "How much time should we look at for the retreat? One day, two days?"

Nodding his head and glancing around the table, Greg suggests, "If we get started early and work diligently, focusing on the matters at hand, one day should be enough. We should be able to finish by supper time."

Roger jumps in, "And speaking of supper time, I believe it is lunch time." He nods toward the waitress approaching their table carrying a large tray with six plates of food.

During the course of the meal, Tim restarts the conversation, this time directed at his staff. "What do you all think about the retreat? I think it will be very beneficial and almost necessary for us to move forward as Greg has explained. I suggest we set aside one Tuesday and get away somewhere. We already use Tuesday for our staff meeting and other meetings. I know my Tuesdays are full of meetings." Tim pauses, looks at Marcy and says, "Marcy, you can make it since you're already here at church on

Tuesdays. It would not require an extra day for you." He stops, realizing something. Tim is respectful of the time his staff puts into their ministry at 4Cs. He continues, "Though I realize you spend part of your Tuesday preparing and doing ministry, probably more so than the rest of us. Could you carve out one Tuesday for the retreat?" Tim knows Marcy is going to say yes to the retreat, but he wants her to know that he understands and appreciates the sacrifice of time she will be giving.

Marcy quickly nods and says, "Yes, of course. I too believe this is necessary for us to accomplish our overarching goal. I certainly do not want us to be spinning our wheels, asking our people to do something for the sake of doing something. When were you thinking, next week?"

"No, probably not next week. That may be a little quick for everyone to change their schedules." Glancing around the table, Tim questions, "What do the rest of you think? Two weeks from today? Could everyone clear their schedule for a retreat that day?" Looking each person in the eye, one at a time of course, Tim calls for a personal response. "Roger, What about you?"

Quick with his response, Roger replies, "Certainly. I don't believe I have anything that can't be rescheduled that day."

Andy responds as Tim's eyes meet his, before Tim can ask the question. "Sure, two weeks from today works for me." Shrugging his shoulders, he continues, "I can probably do next Tuesday as well if needed."

Tim nods in thanks and agreement and says, "That's fine. We'll stick with two weeks if that works for everyone else."

Tim looks to Susan as she responds. "Tuesday is early enough in the week that I can get away. Thursdays and Fridays are my busiest days with set schedules—getting ready for Sunday. So, yes, I can be available that day."

"Good," says Tim with a smile on his face. "That only leaves one, our coach. What about it, Greg? Can you give us that day?"

Greg has been checking his calendar on his smart phone, and just as he finishes typing something, he looks up and says, "Yes, I've got you down. I just put it on my calendar."

Pastor Tim, with a resounding voice of satisfaction, states, "Good, then it is a date. Two weeks from today. I'll work on getting us a place to meet—away from the church."

Roger is the one with a quizzical response this time. "Why? Why away from the church? It seems that if we meet at the church we would have everything we need, and in case one of us needs something out of our office, we just have to run down the hall to get it."

Before Tim can respond, Greg interjects a question of his own. Moving his gaze around the table he asks, "What would be an advantage or advantages of not meeting in the church building?" Greg has taken the opportunity to engage the staff in a teachable moment. (Debrief: *Teachable Moments*)

Susan speaks up quickly to the point: "Distractions. To get away from all the distractions. There are always people stopping by, deliveries, phone calls, all sorts of distractions at the church. We eliminate those by moving somewhere else for the day."

Andy is leaning into the table, looking toward Susan as she speaks, nodding in agreement and says, "I've been at the church on Saturdays and late evenings, and it seems no matter when I'm there, someone stops by or a church member will call. You are absolutely right, Susan. If we meet at the church, we will have distractions."

"Good," says Greg. "That's the biggest one. What else?"

Silence encompasses the table for a stretched-out fifteen to twenty seconds. Marcy looks around the table and begins with a little hesitancy in her voice, not certain if this is what Greg is asking for. "If we're at the church, I know I have a tendency to think of the things I need to get done: cleaning play rooms and straightening up classrooms from Sunday. I'll remember a phone call I need to make or an order to be placed. I guess those are distractions too, but if we're away, my thinking, my focus will likely be more on the retreat topic, instead of the daily routine and order of business." Roger is nodding as he knows his mind runs in a similar fashion. Tim is trying to hide the slight smile on his face as he realizes Greg has successfully led his learners in a teachable moment, a discovery learning teachable moment.

The meal continues with varying conversations around the table. There also seems to be an elevated air of excitement around the table. Greg and Tim exchange glances with a smile as they both know what has happened that day, both in the staff meeting and over lunch. The staff members are sensing a renewed joy for the work of service to which they have committed their lives.

DEBRIEF

ENGAGING THE HIGHER-ORDER THOUGHT PROCESSES

When we study the works of Jesus, we see He was a Master at engaging the higher-order thought processes of those in front of Him, be it disciples, followers, or the Pharisees and other adversaries. What does this term "higher-order thought processes" mean? It is engaging your listeners into becoming life-changing learners, causing them to go beyond mere recall and to delve into a deeper level of thinking and processing information. For learning to take place, one must be able to relate to the topic being discussed. The only way to relate to something is to have some prior knowledge. Learning always builds upon learning, therefore we must always have some prior knowledge related to the topic at hand to be able to understand the new information.

For example, we know an infant, once she develops her motor skills adequately, will transfer everything she picks up to her mouth. Have you ever wondered why? Consider this. What is the very first action where a baby learns satisfaction? It is being fed. When hungry, a newborn knows to cry in hunger. What does Mom do? She instinctively feeds the newborn. The newborn experiences satisfaction. As that baby grows and discovers new things, the only option she knows is to take that new toy, scrap of paper, or other object to the place where satisfaction is experienced. The youngster will only grow out of this as her ability to grow in understanding increases and she is taught other options.

In our story, Greg uses a couple of statements to engage the higher-order thought processes of his listeners. Then, he pauses, allowing each person to assess, reflect, and ponder the stated information. Too often, leaders and teachers jump ahead giving an explanation and not allowing these higher-order thought processes to be fully engaged. In doing this, we lose the greatest learning experience. Greg waits silently for a response. Then when Marcy asks the question for clarification ("What do you mean? What opportunities would we miss?"), Greg still does not give a direct answer. He gives enough to allow those wheels of higher-order thought processes to continue in each of his listeners around the table.

Another tool Greg uses here is also one of Jesus' teaching techniques. He uses an analogy and an object lesson (taking a trip). Why? Because everyone around the table has taken a trip and can relate to the question posed by Greg, "What is the first vital piece of information you need before you can plan or take a trip?" In doing this Greg is able to allow the discussion to flow from the learners before turning the analogy back to the matter at hand. Engaging the higher-order thought processes helps people process the information being offered and transforms it into learning by attaching the new information to what is already stored in the memory bank of our mind. Jesus knew to engage His listeners' higher-order thought processes would bring about life-changing learning—and look at the following He gained as a leader. The teaching techniques He used were geared to learning rather than dispensing information. Learn to use leadership and teaching techniques that focus on learning not teaching. It's what Jesus did, and all His teaching/learning techniques engaged the higher-order thought processes. (For more on engaging higher-order thought processes see *Teaching That Bears Fruit*.[6]

PROBING THE LEARNING AND UNDERSTANDING

Greg could easily have given an answer, satisfied his listeners, and moved the team along in the discussion. However, Greg knows the importance of understanding the learned information. Therefore, instead of answering himself, Greg gives everyone around the table an opportunity to express his or her thoughts about the information being shared. This reinforces the learning experience in the mind and memory bank as each one must engage the higher-order thought processes to be able to relate their findings to Marcy and the others. Without saying, "What did you learn?" Greg is asking each one that very question.

Using questions like this instead of automatically giving the answer also allows a learning experience to come from someone in the room other than the leader. In our story, Marcy may catch the learning experience better and quicker from Roger's own learning experience than through an answer from their coach, Greg. At the same time, everyone else in the room will be evaluating their learning experience with Roger, giving them time to assess and follow up with a comment of their own. Learning builds upon learning, and understanding comes from being able to relate what is being said or taught with what we already know, what is already in our knowledge base. Hearing from different perspectives increases our learning capabilities.

Learn to probe the learning and understanding of your direct reports by recognizing opportunities and asking properly formulated questions. You are not looking to use interrogating questions but questions that engage the higher-order thought processes. You do not always need to give the answer yourself. Remember, people learn best when they discover the answer for themselves. In probing the learning and understanding, you are reinforcing the learning experience, which will lead to more productive output from your team members.

TEACHABLE MOMENTS

Teachable moments are those times when something unexpectedly happens and how you react will teach others around you. I like to say teachable moments are those times you must always be prepared for but you can never prepare for. Jesus knew that when His listeners, disciples, followers, or others were engaged in some activity or debate, they were ready for a learning experience. There are several examples of how Jesus handled these teachable moments. One of my favorites is found in John chapter eight. It is the story of the Pharisees bringing before Jesus the woman caught in adultery. This was certainly an unexpected teachable moment. But who learned in this situation?

First, we know the Pharisees learned something as they one by one dropped the stones they had brought to throw at the woman and sheepishly walked away. Second, there was a crowd, as verse two says, *"all the people gathered around Him."* Whenever Jesus was in public, there always seemed to be a crowd around wanting to hear Him teach and see Him perform miracles. What did those in the crowd learn that day? It is easy to suggest that where Jesus was there also were at least some of His twelve disciples. Apparently at least one was there, John, for he wrote the account of this story. What would you ascertain that His disciples learned at this encounter? And lastly, the woman herself must have learned from this teachable moment. I believe part of her learning was that forgiveness can overcome the law. She received mercy and forgiveness that day, and I believe she walked away a changed woman.

There was another time when Jesus was approached by the Jewish religious leaders and He called them a brood of vipers. Had Jesus responded the same way on this occasion (with the woman caught in adultery), He might have incited some of those present to violence. Instead, He remained calm, collected, and with one exploratory statement allowed them to render their own ruling on the situation. What was His exploratory statement? *"If any one of you is without sin, let him be the first one to throw a stone at her."* It is an exploratory statement as it requires each person present to ask himself the question, "Am I without sin?" and "If I throw a stone, will I be caught in a lie?" Once again, Jesus has engaged the higher-order thought processes of the woman's accusers and the others present that day.

When met with a teachable moment, how we react teaches everyone around. We must always be prepared for teachable moments without ever knowing when or how they appear. Teachable moments lead to discovery learning, as in our story. Many leaders would have jumped in with an explanation and answer to Roger's question. Greg did not give the answer. Instead Greg recognized this teachable moment as his listeners were engaged and ready for a learning experience—a discovery learning experience. Through Greg's leading the discussion and asking the right questions, the staff discovered the answers for themselves. Watch for more teachable moments as our story unfolds. And be sure to watch for the teachable moments in your own life as well. They always create an opportunity for a learning experience.

Chapter 6

Let the Retreat Begin–
Defining the Process

Pastor Tim spoke to John Stewart, the pastor of another church about twenty miles northeast of 4Cs and secured a room for the retreat at John's church, Harmony, named for the community in which it was planted. It is the perfect distance from 4Cs as it is close enough that everyone could arrive there within about a thirty-to-forty-minute drive. Yet it is far enough from home and church to avoid distractions and help everyone focus on the topic at hand.

Tim is the first to arrive. He walks in and heads for Pastor John's office, where he is greeted by the church secretary. Hearing Tim's voice, Pastor John appears in the doorway between his office and the secretary's. "Good morning, Tim. How are you?"

Tim turns around quickly and replies with a big smile across his face. "Great! How are you?"

John nods and says, "I'm great too. Are you ready for today?"

Tim, with a couple of nods of his own, answers, "Yes I am. I am really looking forward to today. Thank you again for allowing us to meet here. We'll return the favor someday if you want."

Actually," replies John, "We might take you up on that. But first I want to hear more about what you are doing. I like what you spoke about on the phone. So I'll be curious as to what you come up with and how you implement it when you get back to Calvert City. Are you ready to see the room you'll be in?"

With a quick and positive twist of the head, Tim retorts, "Certainly, on both counts. I'm ready, and I'll gladly fill you in and keep you updated. Perhaps we can go to lunch in a week or two and talk about it."

Just as they head out the office door, Susan, Roger, Greg, and Marcy enter the church building. After exchanging greetings and introductions to John, they all head down the hallway. John stops and turns the light on in a room halfway down the hallway and says, "I think you'll find everything you need in here." As they enter the room, each one comments on something about the room, such as the conference-type table and cushioned chairs. Pastor John continues, pointing out a couple of items as he speaks. "There's a white board and markers, a coffee pot over here, and I see Roger has a large pad of tear sheets."

Marcy interrupts, "Yes, Roger takes big notes." Everyone enjoys a laugh as Roger nods and swings the large pad in front of him.

John steps outside the doorway, looks and motions to his right and says, "And the restrooms are right next door." Hearing voices come from the other end of the hall, John turns back to his left and says, "And it looks like two more have found their way in." He steps aside, introduces himself, and in walks Andy and another man, tall, thin, apparently in his early forties.

Tim interjects, "Great. Thank you, John, we appreciate it."

Greg takes a couple steps toward the door and the tall thin man that he does not know, and extending his right hand he says, "Hi, I'm Greg, you must be—"

He's interrupted by the man who, extending his hand to meet Greg's, says, "Hi, I'm Joe Greer, chairman of the deacons at 4Cs. Nice to meet you, Greg. I'm looking forward to what you are going to do for us."

Greg is quick to respond, "Oh it's not so much what I am going to do for you. My plan is to lead you as a team to come to the God-honoring decisions that He desires."

Tim is at the front of the room standing with the white board to his back and says, "Okay, are you all ready? Get a cup of coffee or bottle of water if you want and let's start in a couple of minutes."

Roger jumps in, "Wait, before we start I have a question." Everyone stops what they are doing and turns to hear Roger's question. "I'm not sure I can do this. I mean, I'm confused." He pauses, looks around, lowers his head, and with an almost playful painful look on his face says, "I mean, Andy is here five minutes early. That's confusing." Everyone in the room including Andy breaks out in laughter.

As everyone makes their way to a seat around the table, Tim begins, "I want us to begin the day spending time in prayer. We all know without prayer what we do here today is in vain." He gives some instruction to pray for the day's events and topics as well as the church's future. The group spends the next fifteen minutes in prayer, asking for clear, uncluttered minds, God's guidance in all discussions, and a prosperous day in God's eyes. Following the prayer time is a few seconds of awkward silence, but not because of what anyone has said or not knowing how to transition. When a group of people have a time of intervention from God, it produces an awkwardness, a sense of inability of self and dependence on God. This is what everyone was feeling. Until as a group you reach this state, it may be difficult to move forward seeking God's plan for your church. (Debrief: *Steeped in Prayer*)

Tim begins the meeting by thanking everyone for their work and service to the church and thanking Greg for being present to lead the team on this day. Then Tim turns the meeting over to Greg. Walking to the front of the room, Greg thanks everyone for their attendance and begins: "I am grateful for the opportunity to assist you in this process and am looking forward to what God leads you to today and in the coming weeks and months. Today, we are going to have multiple sessions. We'll take breaks along the way, but I would like to hang with one topic until we are finished with it. Okay?" Greg pans the room for everyone's approval of understanding.

"First, I believe we need to understand the parts of what we are going to be working on today. I want us to view this as a journey. Pastor Tim has referred to this as a *turn-around journey*. So, this is our journey. We talked a little about this in the restaurant two weeks ago using the analogy of taking a trip in your car. I want to expound on that idea and dig a little deeper. We are going to spend the day planning the first part of our—your—journey as a church. Let's look at this journey prep.

"When you plan for a journey, the first piece of information you must know is where you are going. I believe Roger reminded us of that at the restaurant. The second is how you are going to travel and what you need to get there, right? Isn't this what we talked about in the restaurant?" Everyone nods in approval—except Joe Greer since he was not at the restaurant. Pastor Tim has briefed Joe and caught him up with what the team has been discussing. Greg continues, "In the church, your ultimate destination is to fulfill the Great Commission, right? This is what you told me that you came up with as a conclusion in your assessments a couple of months ago." Again, everyone is nodding, including Joe.

Greg turns to the white board and on the left side draws a square with a triangle on top and a cross on top of the triangle. Inside the square, he writes *4Cs* and says, "This is you—your church." Then moving to the opposite side of the board (the right end), he writes the word *mission* about the same level as the cross and underneath it he writes the letters *GC*. Turning back to the team he says, "The Great Commission is your mission; it is your ultimate destination, correct?" Everyone nods in agreement. Moving back to the left side of the board, Greg draws a domed box with two smaller circles underneath, depicting a car.

"This is the vehicle you'll be taking to reach your destination. As the church, what is your vehicle?" (Notice the question is designed to probe the higher-order thought processes. Everyone must engage deeper level thinking.)

Marcy speaks first, "It's the people, it's us and our church members."

Greg nods slightly more as a recognition of Marcy's vocalizing her thoughts and says, "That's a good answer; however, if the church is the people as we claim, can the people be both the church [pointing to the drawing of the church] and be the vehicle at the same time?" Silence floods the room, but Greg can see the wheels of their minds turning. He knows they are processing the information.

Roger, the worship pastor, speaks up next, "No, they cannot. However, someone must be driving the vehicle, and certainly there are passengers in the vehicle, right?" he queries, looking at Greg.

"Right," answers Greg. "So how do you as a church make progress on your journey?"

Andy taps the head of his pen on his notepad three times, looks up at Greg and says, "Isn't it what we do, our actions and our ministry?"

Greg is smiling, "Yes it is, Andy. Your vision is your roadmap, and ministry is the vehicle that gets you from here [laying the tip of his dry-erase marker on the church drawing] to your destination," now in a sweeping motion pointing his marker to the other end of the board.

Greg looks around the room and sees some are taking notes, some reproducing the drawing on their notepads. He waits for all to look up. Susan, Tim, Joe, and Andy are all nodding in agreement and understanding. Marcy and Roger have expressions of understanding and wanting to hear more on their faces. Greg senses everyone is in agreement and is following the analogy. "Okay, we have the church. We know your ultimate destination, and we have the vehicle that is going to take us from where we are now to our destination. This trip you are on as a church is not a one-day or even a one-year trip, though, is it?" Greg hesitates, wanting to see the reactions of those involved. The faces of Roger, Joe, and Marcy change to puzzled looks. Greg is satisfied because he anticipated this change of expression and body language. He knows his listeners are ready for a learning experience. He continues. "When will you know you have reached the end of your journey as a church?" he asks while pointing to the destination end of the white board. Everyone's higher-order thought processes kick into gear again. Some are looking at the white board as if it is going to reveal the answer. Greg does not answer but waits in silence for an answer. (Debrief: *Always Wait for a Response*)

"When we reach our goals," states Marcy. "When we see the results of reaching families and making disciples," she continues. Greg's demeanor doesn't change. Instead of commenting, he looks around the room for other responses.

Roger jumps in, adding to Marcy's answer but with an air of question. "When we see all our people engaged in ministry, bringing people into the fold, and not only growing in Christ themselves, but also maturing others, mentoring younger believers in the faith?"

Andy begins to nod, but stops mid-nod, cocks his head to the right and produces a very quizzical look at Roger's statement. Andy then jumps into the conversation, "That doesn't sound right. I mean, it is absolutely what we want and what the church should be. But the more I think about it, it does not answer the question, at least not in my mind."

Joe speaks up for the first time. "I think I know what you mean," he says, looking at Andy, "but can you explain a little more?"

Andy continues, "I believe the question was, how will we know we've reached the end of our journey. We don't reach the end of our journey until God calls us home, right?" He looks around the room for approval from everyone then stops, resting his gaze on Joe.

Moving his head slightly left to right and back again, Joe responds, "But, just because I die, doesn't mean the church dies. It lives on. So where is the end of our journey as a church?" He poses his question to everyone seated around the table.

Roger cocks his head to the left and nods as if to say, "Hmm, he's right. I had not thought about it that way." Marcy and Susan are nodding in recognition of a new-found facet to their thinking as well.

Tim interjects, "I think you two [looking at Andy and Joe] are on the right track. The journey is an ongoing one. What we do in our time at the church, what we are considering today, is but one small part of the journey." Turning back to Greg, Tim asks, "So what are you looking for? How will we know?"

"You've done well," Greg replies, looking around the table to recognize everyone's input. "Your journey as a church does not end. At least not until God says it ends. You have come to the needed conclusion." He turns to the right side of the white board. "All along I have referred to this as your ultimate destination. If you are driving in your car on your journey and you are leaving from Richmond, Virginia and driving to Los Angeles, California, are you going to try to drive it in one day?"

Andy, Joe, and Tim all reply simultaneously, "No." At the same time Roger, Susan, and Marcy all shake their heads in the negative.

Greg continues, "You will likely plan your trip in segments. We often refer to these as legs of the trip; first leg, second leg, and so on. The first leg of your trip might be from Richmond, Virginia to Louisville, Kentucky. Would this be a reasonable distance to complete as one leg of the journey?"

Everyone nods and Roger replies, "Yes, that could be accomplished in one day. It's about a nine-to-ten-hour drive. So it could easily be one leg of the journey."

Greg smiles and responds, "Exactly. Think about what Roger just said. What did he tell us?"

Andy answers, "He told us we could drive it in one day."

Greg probes, "Which is another way of saying...?"

"That it's doable." Andy takes on Greg's probing. "You can't drive to California in one day, but you can drive to Louisville."

Pastor Tim picks up the conversation. "It's breaking the trip down into doable pieces. We must do the same on our journey as a church. We are not looking at the end of the journey, but what the church can accomplish in the next seven months that will move us closer to our destination."

"Exactly," says Greg. "That is what we are looking for and how we must address every aspect of the ministry of the church. If we say or think that to get to a certain place by a particular date we will have reached our destination, is wrong thinking and we will stagnate and die. Unfortunately, we see this too often in churches. It is not necessarily that they believe they have reached the destination. But in too many churches following a period of successful growth and prosperous ministry, church leaders and members sit down and rest on what happened the last five or ten years. And in that kick-back-and-rest period is when decline sets in and the church stops being the New Testament church that Christ ordained."

After a short pause to allow the thought to germinate in the minds of his listeners, Greg continues. "So what we are going to do today is to plan some of the next leg of 4Cs' journey as a church. As a church you must take your journey one step at a time. It is okay to dream and plan for the future, but that is another retreat at a later date." Greg smiles and everyone is smiling with him. "So let's review what we have so far before moving on. We are the church. The church is the people. We know our ultimate destination is to fulfill the Great Commission."

Roger interjects, "That's our directive from God. He gave us the 'ultimate destination' as a church." Tim is smiling and warmed in heart as he realizes Roger remembers the discovery learning lesson in Tim's office almost three weeks ago.

Greg continues, "The first thing we need to do is turn your overarching theme into a goal."

Marcy speaks up, "We said we want to reach, minister to, and disciple families. I thought that was our goal?"

Greg nods and replies, "Well it's certainly headed in the right direction, but it is a theme, something we are willing to focus on; but it is not yet a goal. Can anyone tell me why it is not a goal?" With that Greg pans the room with his gaze.

Roger speaks up, "A goal has to have a timeline, an ending date."

Marcy again jumps in, "We have a date. The objective was to find one thing or theme that we could focus on for the next seven months."

Greg is nodding as he begins his next remark. "You are both correct. A goal has to have an ending date, a timeline, and you have one. In fact, you started with the timeline first. What else is missing?" Silence overtakes the room as everyone engages their higher-order thought processes, pondering the possibilities. Greg observes everyone's posture and body language. Roger, Susan, and Joe are looking down at their notepads. Tim is jotting something on his notepad before looking around the table at the others. Marcy and Andy are staring at the wall above everyone's heads as if trying to see through the wall to an answer on the other side. Truly, everyone is deep in thought.

After what seems like quite some time, Tim clears his throat and begins to speak. "Our overarching theme is not an objective or goal yet because it does not have any quantifiers." He looks at Greg, then looking around the table, stopping to look into the eyes of each person as continues to speak. "Quantifiers are those things that help us to know if and when we ever reach our goal."

Andy can't wait, so he jumps in and says, "They're our targets, so to speak. In archery or any type of shooting, if I do not have a target to shoot at, I'm simply wasting arrows and time. I'm shooting and may never know if I hit anything. What you are saying, Greg, is we need something to shoot at."

Looking at Tim first, then down the table to Andy, Greg states, "Yes. Yes to both of you. We need quantifiers or targets. A goal must have a 'from here' to 'where' by 'when.'" (Here + where x when = goal.) "We know the here, where we are today, or we need to find that out. Then we must determine an achievable 'where.' Where would you like to be or where should you be by a certain date. That is your target, what you are going to shoot for." Greg pauses and scans the room for facial expressions of understanding or confusion. Everyone seems to be sitting forward in their chair, which is an expression of body language claiming "I'm ready for more." Greg continues, "Here is what I want you to do. Take the next five minutes and consider what we need to look at to turn your overarching theme into a goal for the next seven months. In other words, what kind of targets will you need to set in order to know you are moving toward fulfilling the Great Commission?" (Debrief: *Involve Everyone in the Process*)

DEBRIEF

STEEPED IN PRAYER

We wrote in chapter one of the importance of prayer. In my mind, prayer is of such importance that we need to bring it up again. Prayer is vital to the Christian life, and it is critical to leadership in the church, the body of Christ. If as a leader you do not walk the talk, you are demonstrating to your parishioners that you do not truly believe prayer is what the Bible says. Every leader, whether a pastor, Bible study teacher, deacon, elder, and all others must demonstrate that we truly believe that without prayer our efforts are futile. I cannot emphasize enough for you not to take this lightly. Everything you do needs to be steeped in prayer. When you steep a tea bag, you not only dip it once in hot water, you dip it again and again. The more you steep it, the stronger your tea gets. To steep means to soak, immerse until it is drenched and saturated. Treat your prayer life like a cup of hot water and a tea bag. Continue to steep it in prayer. When you believe you have steeped a decision enough in prayer, steep it one more time.

WAIT FOR A RESPONSE

It is natural in our culture to give an answer. I've watched leaders and teachers ask great questions and not allow anyone time to answer, blowing right past a great learning opportunity. Daryl Eldridge has said, "Never ask a question you do not want someone to answer."[7] Slow down and allow time for your team members to process the information and give you an answer. One reason we do not wait for a response is because silence is awkward. Again, slow down, silence is okay. Silence is a great learning tool when used properly. As noted several times in this book, ten seconds of silence can seem like several minutes. That is no reason to give the answer or move on without an answer.

Learn to read the body language and facial responses of your team. If they seem confused or in need of clarification, you may need to restate or reform the question for a better understanding. Asking good formulated questions will bring about learning and will allow your team to assess more possibilities for drawing a conclusion and coming to a right decision.

When the Pharisees brought the woman to Jesus, He asked a question, then He hesitated, stooped down, wrote on the ground and waited—in silence—for their response. Another great lesson learned from our Lord and Savior.

INVOLVE EVERYONE IN THE PROCESS

One of the dynamics of small groups is involvement. Whether you are teaching a Bible study or working with a team like the one in our story, getting everyone involved is important. If you only want yes people, people to rubberstamp your ideas, you do not need a team. You only need a few people who can nod their heads up and down. But if you want and value input, realizing God speaks to others and you may not have all the ideas, then you'll need to use approaches that assist and ensure every person's involvement in discussions and debate. Everyone's involvement carries beneficial results as it engages each person's higher-order thought processes, allows everyone to be heard, produces learning, and brings cohesiveness and agreement through thought and discussion.

Throughout our story, you have read how Greg and Tim use approaches to garner everyone's response. At the end of this chapter, Greg has asked for another one, setting aside time for everyone to think of possibilities. Notice how he continues the conversation and leads the discussion at the beginning of the next chapter.

Chapter 7

Overarching Goal, Part Two

While the group is thinking through their possibilities, Greg walks to the back of the room and refills his coffee mug; stirring in a little creamer, he turns to look at everyone around the table. He is pleased as everyone is engaged in thought—deep thought. Occasionally one of the group will look up at some of the others or jot down a note on their legal pad. After a couple of minutes, he begins walking back to the front of the room. Greg sets his coffee down, waits a few more seconds, then asks if everyone is ready to discuss their ideas. He waits for all six to look up and affirm acknowledgement of his request.

"Okay, good. But before we do that, I would like for you to take the next five minutes and pair up. We'll do it the way you are seated. Roger, you and Marcy, Joe, you and Andy, and Tim and Susan." As a normal reflex, when Greg calls the names of the pairings, each person looks at his or her partner. Some nod, others smile in acceptance as if being chosen for a team on the playground. "I want you to share your idea with your partner. Regardless of how closely his or her idea lines up with yours, you need to listen closely, because you will be the one presenting your partner's idea." Now the facial expressions change. There are looks of hesitation, bewilderment, fear, and even insecurity. "Don't worry," Greg continues, "You will have an opportunity to defend and speak for your ideas. And you are doing this because I also want you to have an open mind to someone else's idea as well and to be able to defend their idea."

Tim moves his chair so he and Susan can discuss appropriately. The others simply adjust in their chairs, turning to pair up and begin discussing. Greg adds, "One of you begin sharing, and I will let you know when to switch. You'll have two-and-a-half minutes each to share."

Greg calls for the switch at the two-and-a-half minute mark. Realizing a couple of the groups couldn't just switch in the middle of a sentence or thought, Greg allows an extra thirty to forty seconds on the back end, so the second person sharing has the time needed to disclose his or her idea in full. Calling the time and bringing the groups' attention back to the front of the room, Greg asks, "Who wants to go first? And remember you are sharing your partner's idea, not your own."

Andy jumps at the opportunity, "I will. Joe's thoughts are that we need to get more of our families involved. So we talked about how to do that and how to measure progress. To measure it, we would need an idea of how many are involved now and how many are involved at the end of the year. That will give us our 'from here to where by when.' How we do it can take on a variety of—"

Greg holds up his hand as a crossing guard stopping someone from crossing the street. "Hang on to that thought. We'll get to the how in a little while. Right now it is the 'from here to where by when' that we want to focus on. And that is a good one. Before we can determine progress at the end of the year about how many people are involved, we must first know how many are involved at the starting point—which is now. I'll look forward to hearing what else you thought of in the how-to portion of our discussion."

Without skipping a beat, Greg turns his head to his right and asks, "Roger, Marcy, which one of you will share the other's idea?"

Roger and Marcy glance at each other. Roger speaks up, "I will. Both of ours were similar. Marcy's thinking we need to measure the engagement of family members, see how many members of a particular family are involved in the different aspects of ministry and growing in their spiritual walk. If we gauge it solely on the adults, Mom and Dad, we will miss the children and thus miss the family unit. Likewise, if we only gauge it on the children, we miss the family aspect of what we are trying to accomplish, and we'll not know if we have made any true progress with our adults and parents. So we believe we need to find a way to measure the actual involvement of family members. Perhaps measuring involvement in Sunday school, ministry activity inside the church, and somehow outside the church as well. This may not be easy but to measure progress we need those indicators."

Greg nods twice and asks, "So what is your 'from here to where by when'?"

Marcy jumps in, "Growth indicators. How do we measure if they are growing and not just more involved? Doing is not automatically an indicator of growth. We don't want to just make people busier."

"Okay," says Greg turning to the white board, "Let's get these down. Andy, speaking for Joe, you said involvement. And Marcy your idea is growth." While speaking, Greg writes two words on the board, *Involvement* and under it, *Growth*. "Those are both good. Let's see what else we have. Tim, what was Susan's idea?"

Tim looks around the table with a smile on his face. "Well, Susan and I had a little discussion about this last week. So perhaps we had a head start on the rest of you."

Marcy cocks her head to the left and asks, "How could you talk about it last week. Did Greg give you the agenda for today and the questions he was going to ask?"

Tim, smiling again, states, "No, but we're talking about how to turn our overarching theme into a goal, and our theme, we said, is to engage families in ministry and spiritual growth. I know what a goal is— remember I've worked with Greg before." Everyone smiles as Tim continues. "So, I knew we would need to know how many families are involved now to help set our goal. Therefore, I asked Susan to locate that information for us.

"While it is difficult to pinpoint that number, Susan and I came up with some things we will give you later," looking at Greg, "in the 'how-to' part of our discussion. So our assessment, our 'from here to where by when' is the number of family units. As a group we will need to unearth what we believe that means; what constitutes a family unit, for our goal purposes, and at what level are we to measure, etc. Bottom line, what we are both saying is family units involved in active ministry and discipleship or spiritual growth."

Greg continued leading the discussion by going back around the table and asking for Joe and Marcy to give Andy and Roger's idea. The discussion continued for another ten minutes before Greg turned to Susan and asked, "Susan, do you have anything to add about Tim's idea or assessment? We know he said the two of you were on the same track, perhaps due to your work last week."

"No, not really." Glancing down at her notes, Susan continues, "But I do see a correlation among almost everyone's idea for our goal—our 'from here to where by when.'"

Greg's interest is piqued. He noticed a correlation as well. But he is interested to hear Susan's take on what she heard and observed. "Okay, what is it. What correlation do you see?"

Susan sits up straight in her chair and, looking at her notes, says, "Well, everyone's answer had to do with numbers. I know you said [looking at Greg] at the restaurant our goal does not have to be numbers oriented, but we all came up with numbers in our equation." Greg is nodding in agreement. The others are nodding in remembering Greg's statement at the restaurant in answer to Marcy's question. Susan continues, "Also, every answer came around to number of families, family members, or households, though we've not settled on what those numbers should be. I mean not the numbers themselves, but should it be by family member, unit, or household. Or should it be about involvement and/or growth, and if so, what involvement or to what degree someone is involved or engaged."

Greg gives a nod of satisfaction and agreement to Susan. "Wow, very good. You took the words right out of my mouth. Do you all agree and see what Susan is talking about?" Greg asks as he pans around the table.

Everyone is nodding in agreement while Marcy abruptly changes her expression to inquiry, "So have we accomplished anything yet? I mean it's like that was a given?"

Greg, looking directly at Marcy, says, "Yes, certainly you've accomplished something. We have the type of equation we need to set our goal, but we do not have the goal yet. That's okay. We're going to do that next. The fact that everyone's response had a similar equation was not just out there, not mere coincidence. It tells me you all have recognized a mutual and perhaps necessary starting point. That's a very good start," Greg affirms the group.

"Next, let's narrow this down a little. Can we come up with an equation that suits what we are talking about?" Greg turns back to the white board and writes *here to where by when*. Under the when he writes *Dec. 31*. "First, we need to find our focal point. The words I have written on the board are *Involvement, Growth, Engaged,* and *Additions*. These are the words you gave as potential key criteria for us to measure. What are we going to measure? In the next seven months, until the end of the year, what do you think will best suit you for measuring spiritual growth and involvement of families in the church? Before you answer that, I want to give our second definitive. Who are we going to measure, family units, individuals, households, or one of the others you have mentioned?" Greg turns to the board and writes the three words on the board.

Roger raises his pen as if to halt the conversation for a point of reference. "Yes, Roger, what do you think?" quizzes Greg.

Roger gives a quick but short left to right movement of the head before answering. "I have a question. Shouldn't we first know the people group before determining the measurement?"

Greg is nodding with a slight smile. "Not necessarily, but I personally believe it is the best course to take. I am a firm believer of getting the 'who' before the 'what.' Before taking off in the church van, you may not know his credentials for driving, but you first want to know who is driving, right?" He looks around the table for approval. Everyone smiles and nods in agreement. "So let's work on the 'who' first. Are we going to best be able to measure family units, or individuals?"

Marcy is quick to respond, "Individuals. It will be easier to measure the progress of individuals than family groups."

Susan looks up from taking notes and states, "Our overarching theme is families. I think we need to focus on families, not individuals."

Nodding in acceptance toward Susan, then looking at Marcy, Greg asks, "How will Marcy's response correspond with our overarching theme to involve and disciple families?" Instantly, a change in atmosphere overtakes the room. Though Greg did not believe his question to be confrontational, sensing that Marcy and others may have jumped into defensive mode, he doubles back. "I'm not disagreeing with you. But if we're going to find the right equation, we need to explore the different angles. When we walk out of here today, you want to know that we've explored the different options to come up with the best possible solution, right?" Greg is not directing his question at Marcy alone, but looking around the table, visually requesting affirmation from everyone.

Continuing, Greg states, "The question is, 'how will measuring the progress and involvement of individuals correlate to our overarching theme to involve and disciple families?'"

After another long twenty seconds of silence, Roger breaks the quiet in the room. "Well, when we—the choir—want to tackle a new piece of music, we break it down and each group learns his or her part. Then when we put the parts together, all the pieces fit in harmony. If we help the individuals in a family, wouldn't we be at least attempting to strengthen the harmony of the family?"

Marcy turns to Roger with a look of surprise and says, "Wow. That's a pretty good analogy. Did you just think of that or have you been waiting to work that in?"

Roger smiles, "No, I just thought of it when Greg asked." Roger looks to the front of the room where Greg is standing.

Greg nods in approval. "That is good." Not wanting to skew the thought of others, he looks around the table and asks, "What else? What are other reasons?" Andy and Marcy both comment on parents leading children while their ministries can lead children and students to understanding their role in the family as well as spiritual growth. The conversation moves around the table as Tim, Roger and Marcy engage in the conversation. Greg then asks for Joe or Susan's input.

Joe states, "I think they've done a good job covering it."

Susan adds, "Yes, I'm good with those reasons, and I agree with them."

"Okay," Greg initiates, "What about family units as a whole. What are some of the reasons we should focus on those instead of individuals? Remember, we want to explore all options."

Roger retorts, "I thought we had settled on individuals. Now I've got to think again." He smiles and everyone smiles with him. (**Debrief:** *Explore All the Options*)

Joe speaks up, "The family is under attack in our nation today. If we can focus on engaging family units, perhaps we can strengthen the bond and relationships within the family and with God."

Andy pushes his lower lip out slightly and with a quick nod admits, "Good answer, Joe. I like that and think that is what we should be about. It could help keep so many of our young adults from wandering away from family values and the church."

Roger quips, "It certainly couldn't do any harm. I agree." Susan, Marcy, and Tim are all nodding in agreement.

"Great insight, Joe," insists Greg. Looking around the table, Greg asks, "What else? What other thoughts do you have?" Andy, Marcy, and Tim take a turn voicing the need for strengthening families through the different ministries of the church, to which the others all agree. The conversation carries on for six to seven minutes more. Once it appears everyone has had their say about families as measuring elements, Greg calls for a question. "Okay, you've given very good responses for defending individuals as a measuring element and family units as well. So which of these will we add in our equation?"

Again Greg leads the team in a lively discussion of the merits of each of the choices before them. There is a healthy debate going, and some in the room actually switch from one option to the other. The debate is healthy because no one is raising their voice. No one is angry or upset with another person's viewpoint. Everyone is engaged in the discussion and fleshing out the possibilities and potential outcomes. (**Debrief:** *Healthy Debate*)

A portion of the debate inside the discussion was the point of view of Marcy, Andy, and Susan that it would be much more difficult to measure the progress of a family unit than to measure the progress of individuals. Joe, Tim, and Roger have all advocated for families as the element for measurement. Marcy states, "How can you measure a family's progress? I know I brought up families, but I just don't see how we can get a quality reading on families as a measurement."

Following ten minutes of this healthy debate, Greg, who had guided the group throughout, takes the opportunity to introduce a new facet through a question. "Marcy, is it possible you [inferring Andy and Susan as well] are looking at traditional measurement devices and Tim, Roger, and Joe may be looking at other, outside-the-box-type measurements?"

"I'm not sure what you mean?" questions Marcy. But around the table, everyone's higher-order thought processes have kicked in. Greg pans the room and waits. Marcy's gaze follows Greg's panning the room.

After a moment of silence, from the other end of the table Joe speaks up, "If we only look at the traditional ways of measuring in a church, I can see where the family unit would be harder to measure." He pauses, looks around the table before continuing, "In the business world, things are practiced every day for one person in the family that affect the entire family. Take insurance for instance. A life insurance policy taken out on a father and husband is for whom?"

Andy quickly quips, "It's for the family. The benefit for the husband is the satisfaction and peace of mind for planning ahead."

"Exactly," says Greg. "Another good analogy, Joe. So what type of measuring elements will that require for you as a church?"

Roger chimes in, "It's going to require more than attendance," noting one of the traditional church measurements.

Tim clears his throat and begins to speak, "Is it possible that we are going to need some measurements of family units and some of individuals?" Looking around the table, Tim realizes most everyone's gaze at him is trying to determine if their pastor is now calling for a compromise.

Though no one has spoken a word, Tim continues, "No listen, I'm not talking about compromise. If a woman brings her children to Vacation Bible School, is she or her family involved? Her children may be, but she is not. Likewise anyone can attend one of our Sunday morning Bible study classes. Their attendance does not mean they are involved, and involvement does not mean they are engaged. If they are engaged, they are doing something and not just sitting in class on Sunday morning. They are taking an active role in and with the class in ministry. I think what we need is a multiplicity of measuring devices that sometimes looks at the family unit and others may include individual engagement."

Greg is nodding as Tim finishes, and everyone turns their gaze to Greg. "You bring up a couple of good points, Tim. The first one I want to hear from you [making a sweeping motion with his right arm to include everyone] about is involvement versus engagement. Can we settle on one of these for the most efficient use for our goal? Which one and why?"

Roger speaks first, "I believe Pastor Tim said it a minute ago. You can be involved and not be engaged. If we really want to measure progress and spiritual development, I believe we must go beyond involvement and look at measurements that assess engagement."

Marcy counters, "But if someone is involved, they are doing something. They are part of the church, right?"

Joe nods and replies, "Yes, they are, but involvement requires little sacrifice and does not require getting out of our comfort zone that we all love."

Roger jumps back in, "I like what Tim often says, 'no learning or growth ever takes place in the comfort zone.' So, I have to agree with what Joe is saying: if we are to expect and measure growth, we must lead for growth, and that will require sacrifice on everyone's part—to grow, I mean."

Susan nods in agreement as Andy says, "I agree. That makes perfect sense to me. I say engagement is the greater of the two."

Greg looks around the table. Everyone except Marcy is nodding. Roger, Tim, and Joe simultaneously say, "Engagement."

Greg, not wanting to leave the topic with someone's mind still wondering asks, "Marcy, what about you? Can you tell us more about involvement and how that can be our element of measure?"

Marcy looks up at Greg, shakes her head and says, "No. They have convinced me. I agree engagement can demonstrate a deeper level of involvement. I'm good with that. We should go with engagement."

Greg looks to his left. "Susan, can you tell us what you found out in looking at families currently involved or engaged in the church."

Susan pulls a sheet of paper out and says, "Yes. As Pastor Tim and I looked at this, we indeed looked at who is involved, and the best I can come up with is that we have seventy-three households represented in our active membership. Of those seventy-three, thirty-eight are here at church at least once a month. If we look at those to see how many are involved in something at church more than twice each month, our number drops to twenty-nine households. So in my opinion, it looks like twenty-nine would be our highest number of households or families involved. And that number is involved, not necessarily engaged."

Andy interjects, "Twice a month isn't very involved—or engaged I mean."

Tim shakes his head and responds, "No it's not, and just a few years ago that would not have been considered active involvement in the church. But as I looked at statisticians and researchers, it seems that to be active in church today twice a month is sort of the norm. I can't say that I agree with it, but it is what society is telling researchers."

"What do you mean?" asks Roger.

Tim replies, "When asked by researchers if they consider themselves or others to be regular attenders of church or active in the church, the responses show people consider themselves to be active and regular if they attend one to two times a month."

Roger is shaking his head in disbelief. "Wow, you're right, that is a change in the last few years."

Greg continues to lead the team in another ten minutes of discussion. At the close of the discussion, the team decides on the following overarching goal: "*To move from twenty-nine families actively involved to forty families actively engaged in ministry and discipleship by the end of the year (December 31).*" One of the key elements coming out of the discussion is the wording of the goal. Notice the wording: "To move from twenty-nine families *actively involved* to forty families *actively engaged* in ministry and discipleship by the end of the year." The team believes moving people from being *involved* to being *engaged* will be an outward evidence of spiritual growth.

"Good job!" remarks Greg. "That's step one. We'll be working on the others the rest of today. And the others should come easier now that we have our overarching goal. Every decision you make from this point on should draw its focus from your overarching goal. Let's call it your OG. Not only today but for the next seven months, you've said your focus will be your OG. Let's take a break. I know we could all use one. Let's be back in fifteen minutes."

DEBRIEF

EXPLORE ALL THE OPTIONS

This is an avenue new to many leaders and teams. In many churches and other organizations, had this conversation taken place, the discussion would have stopped and the team would have moved on to the next topic. Greg, however, leads the team back to the starting point of the discussion in an attempt to explore the other options that might be viable in this situation.

A good thought to remember is that the first option discussed may not be the absolute best for your current situation. Using the right questions to probe the knowledge of everyone around the table will be very beneficial in ensuring you come up with the best solution. In addition, you will be able to inform the whole organization, the church, that you have investigated multiple options before coming to your conclusion. You want to get input from every team member. Every team member and every piece of information each one gives is valuable to the success of the team and the implementation of the process to come.

HEALTHY DEBATE

Healthy debate is a great tool, especially for strategy planning and leadership teams; yet it is one seldom used, or at least seldom used effectively. Healthy debate should work to engage everyone on the team in the discussion. Healthy debate does involve conflict. However, in healthy debate, the conflict always remains on differing points of interest and not on personalities. The scenario played out in most organizations, large and small, is that the conflict quickly turns to personalities. This is detrimental to a healthy outcome. Therefore, it cannot be healthy debate.

Healthy debate is conflicting points of view not personalities. In our story (as in most scenarios), there are differing points of interest, each of which could be validly supported. The discussion should be led in such a way that the team comes to a 'what is best for our situation' answer and substantiates that answer with factual information. It is not based on any personalities or ministry preferences. Greg had actually prepared the team for healthy debate for a full half hour prior to this decision-making discussion. Did you think it odd that Greg had the team divide in pairs to share their ideas earlier? Then he had them present the other person's idea, not their own. What was he doing? He was allowing them to build a defense for the other person's idea, not the person. Everyone's idea was heard and accepted. But by being voiced by a second person, it brought a broader understanding and acceptance for each idea.

There are varying ways to build in healthy debate. The key is to keep personalities out of the discussion—as much as possible. Make no mistake, people's personalities will come out as they share their ideas and thoughts. Otherwise there would not be passion for any particular idea. What we mean by keeping the personalities out is not to allow differing personalities to close off our open-mindedness. As a leader it may be necessary from time to time to remind the team members to look beyond the person voicing the idea and look at the premise of the idea. It is not the personality but the premise that will be implemented. Seek out ways to implement and lead your team(s) in healthy debate. What other discussions have you noticed in the 4Cs story that you could assess as healthy debate? Watch for more in the remaining chapters.

Chapter 8

Destination Indicators

E veryone is back in the room fifteen minutes later, and almost everyone is seated. As Tim and Andy make their way to their seats, Greg begins the session. "Tim, another thing you pointed out earlier that I want to mention was the possibility to use measuring elements that at times will focus on individuals and other times on families. That idea will come into play in this session and the following sessions today."

Tim nods and in jest responds, "Good, I'm glad I can contribute." Everyone smiles and it is evident all are ready to dive into the next round of discovery discussions.

Greg continues, "As we closed the last session, I stated that from this point forward, every decision you make is to draw its focus to the OG, the overarching goal. In the next sessions, we will look at two things: destination indicators and driving gauges. As you start out on any journey, your focus is on the destination. However you choose to travel, whatever mode of transportation and resources you use, your focus is on arriving at the destination, correct?" Greg turns his statement into a question. Everyone nods, and Greg continues with another question. "How do you know that you are making progress on your journey?"

Following a brief hesitation, Roger looks up and says, "You are getting closer."

Greg queries back to Roger. "Tell me more, Roger. What do you mean by that?"

Roger, with somewhat of a look of surprise and an air of doubt in his previous answer replies, "If you don't have as far to go as you did when you started, aren't you making progress?"

Greg nods and continues his line of questioning. "Perhaps, but could that also be simply because you are pointed in the right direction."

Roger, whose posture has been slightly bending forward over the table, now unsure of Greg's quest for information, turns his hands palms up at about a seventy-five degree angle in a motion of emphasis for his next reply, which he forms as a question of his own, looking at Greg. "Well, yes, but you sure aren't going to make progress going in the wrong direction?"

Greg, with a slight smile on his face (to keep tensions eased more than anything), states, "Absolutely, but pointing yourself in the right direction doesn't mean you are making progress, does it?"

Roger thinks to himself, "Okay, I get this one." And he responds with a nod of agreement.

Greg continues, panning the room for input from the others. "What are indicators you look for to know you are making progress on your journey?"

Remembering the conversation from the restaurant Marcy perks up to say, "Mile markers."

Andy jumps in right behind Marcy's comment, "And exit signs for certain cities and roads along the way."

Without looking up from taking notes Susan inquires, "What about landmarks or other places or buildings you know along the way?"

Greg nods toward Susan. "Absolutely. You are all correct. These are destination indicators. As you pass certain mile markers and landmarks, you realize you are fifteen miles closer than you were thirty minutes ago. The same with exits, cities, or landmarks along the route to your destination. Knowing that Tell City is halfway between your point of origin and your destination, when you pass Tell City you know you have made x amount of progress, right?" Everyone nods in agreement. "These mile markers, signs, and landmarks are important to our journey. If on my journey I see a sign for Junction City and I know Junction City is fifty miles out of my way, I might want to stop and make certain I'm still on the right path or road, would you agree?"

Everyone is engaged in this analogy and scenario. Greg is ready now to turn it back to the church's journey. "What might be one indicator you could use on your journey as a church?"

A few seconds of silence passes, then Andy speaks up, "When we're halfway there, to our goal I mean. When we have six new families engaged."

"Okay," Greg replies without an air of agreement. "Let's think on this one for a moment. It is certainly something that can be measured, right?"

Joe jumps in, "As long as you have accurate measurements up front."

Greg nods, "Exactly."

Joe continues, "Right now we do not have an accurate number of engaged families. The numbers Susan provided for us are for those involved, not engaged, correct?" Susan and Tim nod in agreement.

Greg picks up on Joe's train of thought, "So while that number could be a mile marker, there has to be some redefining first."

Marcy looks puzzled and asks, "I guess that makes sense, sort of, for our journey, but if you're at mile marker six isn't that giving you an indication of where you are, regardless?"

Greg nodding to Marcy answers her question saying, "Yes, to use your words, 'sort of.' Will traveling past mile marker six on highway 127 get you closer to your destination if you are supposed to be at mile marker six on highway 32?" Greg pauses. "You see, mile markers by themselves can be misleading. If you are on highway 127 when you are supposed to be on highway 32, yet you are only watching the mile markers, you could end up way off track and miss your destination. Does this make sense?"

Tim pipes up, "Absolutely. And it happens all the time in churches." Everyone nods in agreement.

Though Marcy is not yet satisfied. "But you asked us to name a mile marker."

Greg's next question is simple but queries everyone's recall. "Did I?" He pauses. "Did I ask for mile markers or destination indicators?"

Roger with an exclamation of understanding replies, "Ah. Yes."

Joe at the same time replies, "Indicators."

Andy questions Greg, "But mile markers are destination indicators. You said so yourself."

Greg, with that partial smile, again looks at Andy and says, "Yes I did. You are correct. What you are witnessing is that just because it is a sign on the side of the road, is it a true indicator?" He pauses to allow the information to sink in. Once he senses all minds are engaged, Greg continues. "That same mile marker, number six, is on hundreds of roads around our state. And it is on each road twice: on the northbound and southbound sides of the road. On the eastbound and westbound sides. What does this tell you about mile markers?"

Joe gives the reply, "They're only good when you affirm you are on the right road and moving in the right and desired direction."

Greg's smile breaks a little bigger now. "How can you translate that into your journey as a church?"

Joe accepts this as his challenge to answer. "To use the number of families as a mile marker, we must assess our position within the other destination indicators that we set for ourselves."

Greg is content, but he wants to know that the others have an understanding. So he asks, "Okay, someone else explain that in your own words. Help me out here."

Following a short period of silence, everyone hoping someone else will answer, Andy speaks up. "I think this is what you are saying. So tell me if I'm right. If we set a certain number of families that we want to engage in ministry and maturing discipleship, progressing to that number could be our mile markers. However, along the journey we need to watch for other indicators to insure we are on the right road, so to speak. In other words, we need to track what type of family involvement we have in Vacation Bible School, Fall Festival, discipleship classes, and ministry opportunities outside the church. Am I on the right track?"

Tim wants to speak, but he looks to Greg first. Greg replies to Andy, "Absolutely. These indicators will have to be determined, but that is what we're talking about, using more than mile markers. Tim, I believe you wanted to say something."

Tim nods, "Yes. I agree," Tim says nodding to Greg, acknowledging his agreement with Greg's response to Andy's statement. He continues, "Good job, Andy. One of the mistakes many churches make is focusing on the mile markers without checking other indicators. It gives a false sense of accomplishment. Wouldn't you agree, Greg?"

"Yes. Absolutely," replies Greg. "In many churches, the only focus—if there is focus—is on the numbers, the mile markers. And as we've noted, watching mile markers alone can be very misleading and in fact can lead a church down the wrong road and away from your destination without the church even knowing it, for years." Greg looks at Marcy. "Marcy, does this make sense? Are you on board with us?"

Marcy nods in agreement. "Yes, yes it does, now that you all have spelled it out for me." Greg continues around the table asking everyone the same question as he asked Marcy. When Greg is satisfied that everyone has an ample understanding of destination indicators, he steers the conversation to the next assignment.

"This is what I want you to do. Thinking of your OG, I want you to work with one other person, not the same partner as this morning. I want you to work together to come up with two destination indicators for your journey as a church." Greg pauses to gauge everyone's understanding of the assignment. (**Debrief:** *Greg Pauses*)

"Between now and December 31st, what will you be able to use as destination indicators—those things that you will be able to look at to see if you are 'on the right track' and making progress?"

Roger turns his chair to face Joe, Marcy and Tim pull their chairs toward one another to share together, and Andy positions his chair so he and Susan can work as a pair on this assignment.

Following five minutes of discussion, Greg calls for everyone's attention. He has placed a large flip-chart style tablet on an easel at the front of the room. We're going to write your answers on this tablet to see what we come up with. One of you will share with us verbally and the other one I'd like to come up and write your ideas on the tablet." Greg looks to his left, "Susan, do you and Andy want to go first?"

Andy straightens up in his chair quickly to respond. "Certainly. Susan will write them on the flip chart since her handwriting is better than mine, and I'll share them with you." Greg hands Susan a marker as she heads to the easel.

As soon as Susan uncaps the marker, Andy begins, "We believe one of our destination indicators could be the excitement of people as they engage in ministry both serving and learning. Going back to the analogy of taking a trip, if along the way there is a really interesting landmark that you want to see, you are probably going to not only stop, but perhaps take some photos. And afterwards you will probably share with others what a great experience it was. On our journey as a church, one of our indicators could be how many people are excited about an event or ministry activity after the activity. What are they saying? If after VBS the only thing they're talking about is how good the Kool-Aid was, then we are probably on the wrong road. However, if they are excited and talking about the Bible stories, the new families we reached, the new friends they met, the faces of the children, and the baptisms to come, then we know we are on the right road and heading in the right direction. So that's one."

Everyone's gaze follows Greg's as he turns to see what Susan has written on the board. 'Excited Engagement Exclamation.' Susan looks at the tablet, giving everyone a few seconds to read it, then says, "How excited are they about what they did, and how are they talking about it: excited engagement exclamation."

She recites the phrase as if to say, what else could it be? Everyone enjoys a laugh at the alliteration to which Roger says, "So Pastor, does Susan give you your sermon alliterations? It looks like she's pretty good at it." The laughter continues.

Greg interrupts the laughter to say, "Thank you. If we choose this one, we'll need to identify ways to measure it, and it has potential." Looking at Andy, he continues, "And a very good explanation of how it fits with our analogy of taking a trip and our journey as a church. What is your second destination indicator?"

The conversation continues around the table as each pair reports their ideas for destination indicators for the church's overarching goal (OG). It has taken nearly fifteen minutes for all three groups to give their reports and the ensuing discussions on each idea. When all three groups have reported, there are four ideas written on the flip chart, as two ideas were duplicated. Greg reviews each one by leading the team in discussions of how each could be a viable destination indicator for the church in accomplishing their overarching goal. Let's listen in on part of the conversation for excited engagement exclamation.

"If this is going to be one of your destination indicators, how will it work for you? How will you measure it?" questions Greg.

Andy, who with Susan posted the idea, speaks up, "In one sense it kind of measures itself. I mean, as people get excited about something, they talk about it. So all we have to do is listen."

Roger breaks in, "Yes, but we cannot be at all places at all times with all of our people. We may not be the ones hearing the good reports. We cannot measure what we don't hear."

Andy nods in agreement and says, "That's true. So we need to train others—Bible study teachers, choir members, deacons [pointing to Joe] and everyone we can to let us know when they hear of such a proclamation."

Marcy is slightly shaking her head. "That's almost impossible isn't it? I mean we may hear some, but are we going to hear enough to quantify this as a measurement?"

Greg is pleased with the healthy debate of the conversation. He casts a glance at Tim, who returns the glance, and they both smile, realizing this is good and the team will likely come to a solution fitting for the accomplishment of the goal. Andy responds to Marcy's questions. "What number is viable to make it quantifiable? If we hear of only one new family who is grateful for their experience in Vacation Bible School or some other event, isn't that a measure of success? I mean successful in that we are on the right road. Somehow we got that one family engaged in a meaningful way."

Pastor Tim joins the discussion, "Andy makes a good point. Every positive reaction, every good comment of engagement is a victory a reason to celebrate. It's an indicator that we are moving in the right direction towards our OG. However, if we see or hear of only one, we may want to re-examine our engagement process for the next event or ministry activity, to try and get more victories and more indicators. If at the next event we can get three..." looking at the board, Tim reads "...excited engagement exclamations, we're showing that we not only are on the right road but also that we've kept our foot on the gas pedal, making good time and progress toward our OG."

With that comment from Tim, Greg jumps in. "Hold on, Tim. You are jumping ahead. That's in the next session." He laughs and most around the table chuckle with him.

Marcy, though, with a quizzical look asks Greg, "What do you mean?" Greg nods in acknowledgement. "I agree with Tim in his thinking and analogy, but we'll get to the gas pedal part in our next session."

It's now Marcy who has a smile about Greg's comment and she states, "Oh. I'm a little slow I guess." Everyone around the table smiles or laughs along with Marcy. Marcy continues, "Getting back to Andy's comment, though, I guess I was thinking of a more concrete number or determining factors to know who is impacted in this engagement process."

With a nod of his head, Greg asks Marcy, "I understand. What do you think that might look like?"

Marcy, looking down at her notepad, shakes her head and says, "I don't know. I thought that's what we could look at for an indicator."

Joe comes to the rescue. "Isn't that what Andy gave us? Marcy, you asked for a quantifying indicator and Andy gave us an indicator of at least one." Joe looks around the table as if looking for affirmation. He continues, "I too was looking for a number. When I heard Andy's comment, I thought, *'Okay maybe. That is one possibility.'* But when Pastor Tim said, 'Every positive reaction is a victory, a reason to celebrate,' it all clicked for me. Ever since Pastor Tim became our pastor, he's been saying in almost every deacons' meeting, and other meetings I've been in with him, that we should celebrate all the victories, big and small. Each positive reaction to someone engaging in ministry is a victory."

Everyone around the table is nodding in agreement. "That's right," says Roger. "Pastor is always telling us the same thing as a staff too. So I think a factor of one is our quantifier for Susan's excited engagement exclamation." Susan looks up from taking notes and smiles. Everyone smiles along with her.

Tim adds, "As long as we are looking for more than one. One is only our base quantifier. Our goal should be as many as possible. Otherwise we'll never reach our OG." Everyone agrees.

Greg is satisfied and asks, "Any other comments before we move on?" With none stated, Greg moves on to the next destination indicator and prompts a discussion.

Twenty minutes later, Greg is wrapping up the discussion for the four destination indicators listed on the flip tablet, excited engagement exclamations, Vacation Bible School, ministry projects, and discipleship participation. (**Debrief:** *A New Measure*) "Another good job to all of you. I think it is time for lunch. I saw Pastor John stick his head in the door a minute ago." Looking at Tim, Greg continues, "After lunch we'll get back to the gas pedal and we will look at our driving gauges." Greg, with a sweeping motion of his right arm, palm up towards Tim, turns the meeting over to Tim for lunch instructions.

Placing his pen on his notepad, Tim looks to the team members. "Pastor John did indeed look in to let us know lunch has been delivered. He and his secretary will be joining us for lunch. Before we go to lunch, though, let's spend a few minutes in prayer. Not only praying for the food, let's pray for what we have accomplished this morning and what we yet need to discuss the rest of our time here today and that we will leave here with clarity and focus. We need to pray that in the days and weeks ahead we will serve diligently putting into place and practice that which God desires, not those things of our own choosing."

DEBRIEF

GREG PAUSES

Notice the number of times Greg hesitates or pauses after asking a question or giving new information and assignments. Many leaders and teachers move through these concepts missing the opportunity for understanding and true learning to take place in the minds of listeners. A pause for even a few seconds will enable the higher-order thought processes to kick into gear, allowing the listeners to process and grasp what is being said. When listeners are allowed the opportunity to engage the higher-order thought processes, the new information is processed alongside familiar information stored in the memory bank of the brain. It is the combining of the old familiar with the new information that brings about understanding and learning.

By moving along in a group discussion or a one-on-one conversation without these pauses, there are few indicators that the person(s) have gained an understanding of what you desire from them. Unfortunately, I've witnessed too many leaders who did not allow this time for understanding, and when the later actions of the listeners did not meet the desires of the leader, the only person held accountable was the listener. In my opinion, the leader is most at fault in many of these situations.

Another error I have seen leaders make is to run through their spiel letting their listeners know what they want without any pauses. Then at the very end of the discourse, they ask something like, "Have you got that?" In most scenarios, the subjects would simply say yes or "I think so," whether they do or not. For this we could find fault with the subjects or listeners. We might ask, why didn't she speak up? All too often though, people have been put down and made to feel inferior enough times that they are willing to risk going into the project with a partial knowledge of the assignment than face scorn and ridicule even if it is subtle and unknown by the leader. For others, they do not speak up and ask questions because they do not want to feel like the only one who does not understand, and they do not want to prolong the meeting.

Practice using pauses in all your discussions and conversations. See what changes come from the people you speak with and those you lead by allowing information to be processed for better understanding. It may seem awkward at first, but you will see positive results. And if the understanding isn't at the level you expect, you can clarify and make any corrections before leaving the discussion, avoiding potential downtime and damage in the ministry field or workplace.

A NEW MEASURE

To some, the idea of using excited engagement exclamations as a destination indicator may seem odd and perhaps not a good measure. Let me suggest it may seem difficult to measure because we have not used measurements like this in the past. We are used to our traditional measuring sticks, attendance and income. Or as some have noted, butts in the seats and bucks in the plate.

People talk about one of two things: that which they are excited about or that which they dislike. While gauging people's conversations may not be a destination indicator for every church, the team from 4Cs realizes great potential for accomplishing their OG. When people are talking positively about results from an event or other happenings in the church body, it is a good indicator the team chose the right path or road for their journey. On the other hand, if there is negative talk, the team has decided to listen and be flexible in making necessary course changes.

It's time we as church leaders began thinking outside the measurement box and leading our people to do the same. Thom Rainer and Ed Stetzer, in *Transformational Church*, discuss the need for a new scorecard.[8] They are not suggesting we reinvent the wheel. Rather, as churches we need to look at what really matters in changing lives. Are we making a difference and what difference are we making? How is that difference transforming lives and reaching more people? Do not be afraid to think outside the box. Then ask yourself certain guided questions as did the team members from 4Cs. Those questions should lead you to understand you are not settling for good when you can achieve greatness through the Holy Spirit.

Chapter 9

Driving Gauges

Following lunch, the team members and Greg filter back into the meeting room, checking e-mail and personal messages and engaging in casual conversation. Once everyone is seated and prepared, Greg takes his place at the front of the room. "All right, that was a good lunch. Now we need to make an extra effort to keep our creative hats on for this next couple of hours. First, let's look at what we have so far." Everyone around the table nods showing they understand what Greg means about making the extra effort to focus following lunch.

Greg continues. "In our analogy we have said that you understand your mission is to fulfill the Great Commission—this is your destination. God set this as your directive as a church. You came to this conclusion in your assessment back in April, correct?" His question was about the Great Commission being the church's mission more than it was about the date. "Your vision also plays a big part in this and you're articulating your vision for the next seven months through this process. Vision is how you are going to get to your destination, how you are going to fulfill your mission. It is your course of action, which is fulfilled through ministry. Ministry, we've said, is the vehicle you will be traveling in—your car for the journey. Your vision is your roadmap to get there." Greg pauses, allowing time for the team members to draw the mental picture he is painting with this analogy.

"We have not talked about your core values, but I know you worked on those earlier this year. Every action you take is an outward manifestation of your core values, right?" He pauses. Tim answers yes while most of the others nod in agreement. "Your core values are the fuel for your journey. If you do not have the correct fuel or enough fuel in your vehicle, you will have difficulty reaching your destination. This is why it is important for you to have and know your true core values."

Pastor Tim interjects, "I had Susan print off a copy for everyone. I know you already have them, but I thought it would be good to have a copy with us today." As Tim is speaking, Susan passes out a copy of the core values document to everyone around the table.

Greg continues, "Today we have set your OG, your overarching goal for the next seven months, this next leg of your journey. And in the session before lunch, we set four destination indicators. Destination indicators are those mile markers, road signs, and points of interest we use to verify that we are on the right road and making progress on our journey. Are those the only four destination indicators you will use?" Greg sees different looks on the faces around the table. Some perplexed, some not sure, at least one trying to determine if this is a trick question.

Following a long five seconds of silence, Roger speaks to the question, "No, along the journey, we may see something that we did not anticipate, yet it could remind us that we are headed in the right direction."

Greg nods with that partial smile of his and says, "Thank you, Roger. Yes, even if we have traveled the journey before, there are always things along the way that we have forgotten about or things that we did not anticipate, yet reveal we are heading toward our destination."

Andy can't contain himself as an apparent light bulb just turned on over his head. "Like seeing a billboard advertising a custom car show in your destination city, and you keep passing or being passed by several old custom-built cars heading in the same direction you are. You realize they are likely heading to the car show." Everyone enjoys a good chuckle and nod in agreement before Greg continues.

"Yes, that would be one. In this next session, we want to look at our driving gauges. If you remember at the restaurant a couple of weeks ago, you told me that the other things you watch on a trip or journey is the gauges on your instrument panel, correct?"

Everyone nods and Marcy replies, "Yes."

Greg inquires of the group, "Tell me what these gauges are that you watch and how they affect your journey."

Marcy looks at Roger and they both look across the table to Andy, which in turn for whatever reason causes everyone else's gaze to follow. Andy looks up, and turning his left hand over, palm up, queries, "What? You want me to go first?"

Roger and Marcy are smiling as Roger states, "Why not?"

Andy puts his pen down, looks toward Greg, and begins, "Well, you pay attention to your speedometer because it tells you how fast you are traveling."

Greg pans the room and says, "Okay, what else? Someone else share."

Roger interjects, "I thought Andy was going to carry this one, not just give us one gauge."

Greg shakes his head. "No, remember we all have to keep our creative thinking caps on. We need input from everyone."

Joe is next to speak up. "You watch your gas gauge to make sure you have ample fuel for where you are headed."

With one nod of the head Greg agrees and says, "That's two, another one?"

Marcy jumps in, "Well, the only other gauge I can remember on my car is the one that tells you your car is not running too hot."

Roger tries to clarify, "You mean your temperature gauge, to make sure your car isn't overheating."

"Yes," says Marcy, "That's what I said, isn't it?"

"Yes, it is," leads Greg. "Roger, what else do you watch on your journey to gauge your progress?"

Roger pauses, purses his lips, then shares, "Well, I watch my odometer to see the miles clicking by. It tells me how many miles I've traveled and gives me an indication of how many more I have to go."

Greg looks to his left, "Susan, do you have one you want to share with us?"

Susan looks up shaking her head. "No, I can't think of any other gauges on my car. I have lights that come on when something isn't right, but not gauges."

Greg nods and smiles at Susan. "That's good. Those are important on the journey, are they not?" he asks looking around the table. "If one of those lights comes on, you realize there is something potentially wrong, not necessarily with your journey, but with your vehicle." Greg pauses to let the minds of his listeners capture the thought. Following a five-second pause, he continues with a question: "What does our vehicle represent on our journey?"

From opposite ends of the table, Joe and Tim both simultaneously say, "Our ministries." Tim expounds, "Our ministries are the vehicle taking us toward our destination."

"Correct," spouts Greg. "And like the lights on your dash panel, in ministry we often call these red flags." Looking at Tim, Greg asks, "Have you ever had red flags in your ministry?"

Nodding, Tim says, "Yes. Boy, have I."

Roger jumps in. "I think we all have, haven't we?"

Marcy is nodding with most everyone else and gives input. "I get it. I see how those 'red flags' we experience are like the trouble lights on the dash of a car. When you see one come on, whether it is a light or a red flag, you need to stop and have it looked at. If you don't, it could keep you from your destination."

Greg is beaming at the discussion and Marcy's input, but before he can speak, Tim interjects, "That is discovery learning in action. Great explanation, Marcy!"

Greg is ready to move the group deeper in their discovery experience. "Let me ask you this." It is obvious his question is for everyone in the room. "Are your driving gauges solely on the instrument panel of the dash in your car?" Silence overtakes the room. This question requires thought because it causes everyone to change their directional thought processes. (**Debrief:** *Changing Directional Thought Processes*) The silence this time is prolonged. Some are puzzled at the question, others unsure. After a time, Greg himself breaks the silence to rephrase the question, thereby releasing some of the tension of the moment. "What else, besides the instrument panel, do you use to gauge where you are at this moment in the progression of your journey?"

Following another seven-to-eight seconds of silence, Roger confidently shares, "Your mirrors. You watch your mirrors. They do not show where you are going, but they do allow you a glimpse of where you've just come from, your immediate past."

Greg nods in agreement and asks, "Okay, how does that help you on your journey?"

Roger is thinking before replying to Greg's question. "It shows you if something is coming up behind you. You might need to get over—"

Andy jumps in, "Or you might need to speed up if you are holding traffic back."

Roger continues, "Using your mirrors can help you determine if you need to make certain adjustments." Greg can see the lights coming on in people's eyes as the thought patterns have shifted away from the dashboard.

Joe joins the conversation. "What about the road in front of you? You watch the road for corrections and things to avoid—potholes and curves."

Marcy interjects, "Right, you do not look three miles down the road. You can't. But you can look at the road 100 feet in front of you." Marcy has a confidence and authority in her voice greater than normal. "When my dad was teaching me to drive, he always said, 'Watch the road 100 feet in front of you and you'll be able to see 500 feet around you.' That's the area you can adjust to, what is right in front of you, not three miles down the road."

Susan stops writing and looks at Greg, "So are you telling us that these driving gauges we need to determine are those things that we can look at any time along our journey and make needed adjustments?"

Greg tilts his head slightly to the left and says, "Well, sort of. I mean, yes, they do, but that's only part of it. Marcy, you used the example of learning to drive." Turning his attention to include everyone, he asks, "When you were learning to drive, how did all of these gauges or visual points come into play? How were you instructed to use them all as you drive?"

Motioning to Greg with his hands, Roger speaks up, "You just said it. We were taught, or at least I was, to use *all* of them. You look at the road ahead, glance to your rearview mirror, side-view mirrors, then your dashboard, and back to the road ahead. If you ignore any one of them, you might miss something that will adversely affect your journey."

Joe adds to Roger's comment, "Each one gives you a different perspective or a particular measurement about your progress on the journey."

"True," says Andy, "Your speedometer tells how fast you are going, your gas gauge tells how much fuel you have, while your mirrors show what you have just passed on the journey, and the road ahead shows how you need to adjust in the immediate future."

Marcy jumps in, "They all tell you something different, yet they are all important for your journey." Greg is tapping a marker on the table in front of him and confidently nodding with that half smile of his. Inside he is sensing victory. *The team has caught it!* He senses they are ready to move into discussion discovering the driving gauges they will use on their journey.

"Great," says Greg. "Here's what I want you to do. I'm going to get you up out of your seats to get the blood pumping a little after lunch. Tim, why don't you pair up with Joe. Andy, you and Roger, and Susan, Marcy, we'll let the ladies hang out together on this one." Tim moves to the end of the table where Joe is seated. Andy and Marcy trade seats, and everyone stands up for a quick stretch. Once everyone is seated again, Greg gives the assignment.

"As a team of two, you will come up with two driving gauges for your journey the next seven months. Remember, a driving gauge is something that you can look at any time during the journey and get an instant reading of where you are, how you are doing, and any adjustments that may need to be made. Everyone got it?" Heads nod around the table. "Good. Go for it!"

About a minute into their discussions, Greg announces, "Keep in mind that in your car, anyone riding with you can use the same gauges. Any one of your passengers can look ahead, behind or check your instrument panel as well as you can. The driving gauges you choose should be identifiable to others as well."

Marcy lets out a sigh. "Oh, that puts a twist on it. I had not considered that." With that, the group discussions proceed. All three discussion groups are going strong at the five-minute mark, so Greg allows them to continue on. Greg is walking around listening in on various conversations and asking or answering questions as they arise.

Nearly ten minutes have gone by before Greg calls for the team's reports. Once everyone is facing the front of the room, Greg begins the debrief session. "Again you will report as a team on your thoughts and give your ideas. One person will write on the flip chart while the other takes the lead in explaining your ideas." Looking to Marcy and Susan, Greg says, "Ladies first."

Susan stands to go to the easel and Marcy clears her throat before beginning. "First, we looked at the speedometer. Your speedometer tells you if you need to speed up, slow down, or maintain your current speed. In our journey, we need to watch our people, the members. Are they following along? If not, do they understand what we are trying to accomplish? Gauging our people will tell us if we need to speed up, slow down, or maintain our current speed." She finishes by looking at Greg and almost turning her last statement into a question.

"Okay," says Greg. "That is a good start and a good use of our analogy of a car speedometer. What comments do you have?" Greg asks waving his right arm around the table.

Roger raises his hand, "I have a question. I do not disagree. I think that is a good idea and needed. But how do we gauge or measure our member's response to our OG?"

Greg fields this question himself. "You bring up a good point, Roger. One thing we need to understand about driving gauges is that each one is an indicator of a particular part of the journey right now, in the present.

And each gauge has a predetermined set of actions, reactions, and adjustments that can be made. Each time you identify what the gauge is telling you at the moment, you choose one of the adjustments and continue on your journey. For this particular scenario, [motioning toward Marcy] 'Are the people following and understanding' is our speedometer. If they are not following as you expected, this is not necessarily a reason to stop and regroup. You may simply need to decrease the speed at which you are traveling. It is like traveling along at fifty-five miles per hour and coming up on a small town with a thirty-five mile per hour speed limit. What will you do—or what should you do?"

Roger volunteers, "You slow down."

"Right," continues Greg. "But it wasn't your speedometer that told you to slow down. Looking ahead you saw a speed limit sign. Reading your speedometer gave you the indicator that you need to slow down. You see, those reactions and adjustments we're speaking of oftentimes come from reading more than one of your driving gauges. And that is why you set more than one gauge. If two or more of your driving gauges give you indicators for needed adjustments, then your options for adjustment narrow and make your job of deciding easier."

Andy raises his hand gesturing toward the flip chart where Susan has written *Fellowship*. "We discussed that one as well," says Andy. "But we said whether or not people are following is gauged when you look in the rearview mirror. I agree, it tells you how to adjust your accelerator, but to gauge if they are following, you must look in your mirrors."

Greg is nodding. "That is a good point and a good indicator as well as a good analogy of seeing where you've just come from. Using that analogy, when you look in your mirror and see they are following at a lagging pace, is that a reason to stop and go back for them?"

Silence takes over for only a couple of seconds before Joe speaks to the question. "No. If you are driving in a caravan of vehicles and the ones behind you are not keeping up, you don't stop. You slow down, back off the accelerator, and allow them to catch up. That's why your mirrors are important on this journey. It only takes a glance to see who or what is behind you. Then you can make the necessary adjustments."

"Right," replies Greg. "And the point is not whether it fits better as a rearview mirror or speedometer. I believe you have identified one of your *driving gauges*. The important thing is not whether it is a mirror or speedometer, the important thing is the adjustment you make in the wake of reading your driving gauges. Do you see the difference?" He pauses, panning the room for assessment and agreement. "Remember, driving gauges give you important data for making necessary adjustments in the moment, not waiting until you are ten miles or ten weeks down the road and by that time way off track. It is about making adjustments immediately to keep you on track." Almost simultaneously, Tim, Andy, and Roger sit back in their chairs sharing an air of confidence with the others around the table. It is not verbalized, but the look on everyone's face is that of confidence. This air of confidence stems from the thought process that this discussion is positive and the team is making progress, which will lead to good actions for the church.

Greg looks to Marcy and says, "We will discuss how you will use that on your journey in our next session. Right now I'm interested to hear your second driving gauge." Marcy nods and begins, "Our other driving gauge you might say pertains to the road ahead. As staff members and other leaders in the church ministries, we need to be watching the road ahead in order to make needed adjustments before it's too late. If we're in the middle of Vacation Bible School and we know there is a big storm brewing coming our way, we need to make adjustments and move inside. Likewise, if we have an event planned, yet our registration is low, we need to make adjustments. Too often I think when we see something like that, we just back off and start cutting corners."

Greg inquisitively interrupts Marcy and asks, "What do you mean? What kind of corner cutting takes place?"

Susan picks up the conversation, "We start cutting our food order."

Marcy jumps right back in, "And we cut the staffing for nursery. Things like that, always cutting back—"

Roger, with a quizzical look jumps in. "What's wrong with that? I think that's good. That's being frugal. It's good stewardship."

"Is it?" questions Marcy. Then she expounds on her thoughts. "The first thing we do is start cutting back, when we should be praying. And before we pray asking God to bring us more people, we need to pray asking God's forgiveness. Asking Him to show us where we have fallen or more likely where we have jumped ahead of Him, trying to do it our way. I just think we don't give God the opportunity to work in maybe the final hours to produce that miracle." Marcy pauses, looking at Greg, then over to Susan, hesitant to look at the others in the room, perhaps in fear that she may have offended them.

To her surprise, Joe speaks first. "That's pretty hard hitting, Marcy. But you are exactly right. We say we love God and He has the power to do wonderful things, even miracles, yet we do not give Him the opportunity. I'm guilty, Marcy. Thank you for showing me that, or allowing God to speak through you to show me."

Andy is chomping at the bit to get in the conversation. "Wow, Marcy, you are right. As you were speaking, the Holy Spirit convicted me of doing that very thing two weeks ago when I cancelled the youth trip for this coming Saturday because of lack of participation. I didn't give God a chance to work in any of those kids' lives." Silence pervades as conviction takes hold of hearts in the room.

After about fifteen seconds, Greg states, "I think this would be a good time to stop and pray. I'll lead—"

Pastor Tim interrupts, "No, Greg I appreciate that, but I'll lead in the prayer. I have allowed this to happen on my watch as Pastor. I am responsible—"

Marcy tries to interrupt, wanting to take the burden off Tim, but he refuses to yield the floor. Holding out his hand as to stop traffic, he says, "No Marcy, God convicted me too just then. He used you to convict us, and we need to repent and ask for His guidance. Let's pray."

As everyone bows, Pastor Tim and Andy both slip out of their chair and bow on their knees. Before Pastor Tim begins his prayer, Joe joins them on his knees as well.

Tim's prayer: "God Almighty, You are so powerful and righteous. We are so fallible and feeble. You have made known to us this hour of one of our acts of unrighteousness. Forgive us, Lord, as we look to You now with humble hearts and teary eyes. We have tried to do something in our own power, thinking it would please You. On more than one occasion we have run ahead of You. Help us each one to learn from this today, to trust You more fully in everything. Not to cut until you say to cut. Not to back off until You say to back off. But instead to seek You and trust You that in all things You have the power to overcome what we see as stopping points. When in reality, they may very well be Your proving points. Forgive me, for as Your leader, Your undershepherd, I have…" Tim continues in his prayer.

When he finishes and says Amen, he is ready to rise from his knees, but immediately from across the room, Andy's voice begins praying aloud. When Andy finishes, Joe voices a similar prayer of repentance and asking for guidance. The prayer then moves around the table. Every person in the room voices a similar prayer.

Greg closes the prayer time, thanking God for His wonderful work in the moment. As the prayer time ends, some are weeping. Pastor Tim steps over to Marcy, gives her a hug, and thanks her for her obedience in sharing with the group. Then unexpectedly, he makes his way around the room, hugging everyone individually, thanking them, and asking for their forgiveness. (**Debrief:** *Showing Vulnerability as a Leader*)

No one had expected this experience when they first bowed for prayer. But everyone in the room understood this was a Holy Spirit moving experience. Greg stands and says, "I think this is a good time to take a break. Let's take ten minutes and come back so every group can share your driving gauges.

DEBRIEF

CHANGING DIRECTIONAL THOUGHT PROCESSES

Greg has been leading the discussion using questions and statements to engage the team's higher-order thought processes. With this question, "Are your driving gauges solely on the instrument panel of the dash in your car?" Greg is forcing the team members to unearth a different line of thinking. It is like a train changing tracks. This question causes the team to think of gauges as something other than instruments found on the car's dashboard. It is a think-outside-the-box question. Greg realized the members were focused only on those instrument panel gauges. So he uses a question to redirect their thinking. The question is worded in such a way that it interrupts everyone's thinking, but it also interrupts their thought processes. After giving time for those thought processes to be broken down, Greg rephrases the question to enlighten his listeners and to reengage their thinking. He could have asked the second question first and avoided the awkward silence. However, Greg knew he needed to break down the thought processes and, after the appropriate time, regenerate them. What do you think, was he successful? The next paragraph demonstrates he was. The conversation changed directions as the team members realized there was more to be explored than the twelve inches of a dash panel.

Changing directional thought processes takes people deeper in their learning experience, causing more than impressions to be made. Changing directional thought patterns does not stop with attaching old information to new. It leads people in a discovery of what they had not considered or experienced in the past. Learning to use questions that change directional thought processes is a powerful tool in helping others gain insight and change behavior patterns (people begin looking at subjects from a different perspective). However, a word of caution is due here. Using this directional change too early or with wrong timing can have a detrimental effect on the learning process. In leadership, this can have an adverse effect on the team's ability and willingness to carry out assignments. Learn to use this when appropriate, but always use cautiously and with wisdom.

Jesus used this type of leadership with the religious leaders, His disciples, and others following Him. Can you name a time Jesus changed the directional thought processes of 1) the religious leaders (Pharisees, Scribes, Sanhedrin), 2) His disciples, or 3) one or more of His followers?

SHOWING VULNERABILITY AS A LEADER

We all have areas of vulnerability. Successful leaders understand that vulnerability is a strength, not a weakness as some would assume. Many leaders want to hide their vulnerabilities, living behind a facade. Researcher and author Brene Brown says, "Vulnerability is actually the courage to show up and be seen." She goes on to say, "Vulnerability is the absolute heartbeat of innovation and creativity. There can be zero innovation without vulnerability."[9] Great and successful leaders understand that revealing their vulnerabilities can bring out the strengths and creative genius in others. Revealing vulnerabilities as a leader also demonstrates you are human and will allow team members not to try to live above their own abilities and vulnerabilities. However, team members will be encouraged to reach to their potential skill and abilities.

If Christ allowing Himself to be arrested, severely beaten, and hung on a cross isn't demonstrating vulnerability, then our dictionaries have the wrong definition. God Himself through Jesus Christ demonstrated the ultimate vulnerability so you and I can have life eternal. Learn and practice vulnerability in your leadership circles.

Chapter 10

Building in
Friendly Accountability

When the team reassembles in the room ten minutes later, Greg calls for Marcy and Susan to take up the conversation where they left off. Marcy picks up the conversation. "Well as you are driving, looking at the road right in front of you, you make small adjustments pertaining to what you see. You might turn the steering wheel to the left or right slightly, accelerate, decelerate, whatever is needed right then at the moment. As a staff, we need constantly to be asking the right questions. That's the only way we can make the necessary adjustments." Following a couple minutes of discussion, the team agrees that the second driving gauge is for the staff to weekly ask the right questions (to be determined later) and to pray together about the progress of the journey.

Greg offers, "Those are two good driving gauges: followship and staff asking questions and praying together weekly. This is the important part of the driving gauges. I think you've got it, but let me emphasize it one time. Every one of the driving gauges lets you know what adjustments you need to make right now, in the immediate. An important part to remember about the driving gauges is not only what they tell you, but how you react immediately. As you are driving, you do not ask yourself questions like, 'Do I pull the steering wheel left or right?' Your mind knows what is needed and you react accordingly. Asking questions is the gauge. Your reaction or response is similar to the action of turning the steering wheel."

Everyone is nodding in agreement with Greg's explanation as he looks to Andy and says, "Andy, Roger, you're next. What two driving gauges do you have for us?" Roger moves to the flip chart to write, and Andy begins. For the next twenty minutes, the group listens to and discusses the remaining four suggested driving gauges from Andy, Roger, Tim, and Joe.

Following the discussion, they settle on four driving gauges they will use in the next seven months. They are these: followship; staff weekly asking the right questions and praying together; are we manifesting our core values and fulfilling the Great Commission; and making personal visits. Greg immediately leads the team in a discussion on how they will use each of the four driving gauges.

"How will you gauge *followship*?"

Marcy cocks her head to the right and asks Greg, "Doesn't that involve asking the right questions as well?"

With a nod of the head Greg replies, "In a sense, yes. All of these driving gauges and your response depends heavily on the right questions being asked by you, the leaders. However, you can also put some ideas in place to help you measure certain things, like followship. What are some of those measuring devices for followship?"

Automatically, everyone's thought processes engage. It doesn't take but a few seconds before Roger breaks the silence. "Our numbers. We already take attendance in pretty much everything we do: Bible study, worship, Vacation Bible School, choir, etcetera. Reading and evaluating our numbers will give us one indicator."

Greg looks at Roger and asks, "Okay, how and when are you going to use numbers to determine followship and whether or not you are making progress with your overarching goal?"

Roger is ready with an answer. "At our staff meeting every Tuesday. We're all there. We can look at the numbers and see if adjustments are necessary."

Tim is shaking his head. "I think that is too late. I agree we should look at them in our staff meeting, but if it happened during the weekend, even if it is Sunday morning, could not waiting until Tuesday be similar to you not being able to see it in your rearview mirror any longer?"

Andy questions Tim. "But Marcy isn't here on Monday. Are you suggesting we get together on Monday?"

Tim tilts his head slightly left then in the same motion straightens it back and says, "We could. But what else could we do?" Silence pervades again as everyone reengages their thought process trying to assess what Tim is asking.

Susan answers with a statement, and then poses a question. "The numbers are on my desk when I come in on Monday morning. That means they are available on Sunday, after each service and Bible study. So could someone look at them on Sunday?"

Though Susan is looking at Tim, Roger intercepts the question. "Sometimes I do look at them before I leave Sunday evening, but there's nothing you can do about it on Sunday evening."

Joe is shaking his head. "I tend to disagree. Is it because nothing can be done on Sunday evening, or because no one has ever thought to assess the numbers and take action on Sunday evening?" All of the staff members are reluctant to answer, because they know the answer.

After a time of quiet reflection, Tim gives the obvious answer. "No one has ever considered looking into it on Sunday. We've allowed ourselves to put Sunday in a box, and we do not think outside that box. I'm not blaming Roger. I've done it too many times."

Greg picks the conversation up. "Tim, you asked, 'couldn't waiting until Tuesday be too late?' Tell us what you were thinking."

Tim takes a few seconds to gather his thoughts. "I guess I was thinking exactly what Joe brought up. I was thinking more about Monday, but as long as they are ready on Sunday, what can we do Sunday? We're not going to come up with all the answers, but we can look at them and begin praying and thinking through the needed adjustments—or celebrations, right?"

Marcy inquires, "Could we have someone put all those numbers on one sheet and make a photocopy for each one of us and put them our mail baskets? We could make a point to look at them before we leave Sunday evening."

Roger has a question of his own adding to Marcy's reply. "Do you think we need to get together on Sunday evening?"

Tim is ready to field Roger's question. "I don't believe we need to get together to meet about it, unless there is something that really stands out, something that needs addressing right then. We all have at times other things to do after the service on Sunday evenings. We go out to eat with other member groups, or activities [pointing to Andy] as well as occasional team meetings. I wouldn't want us to sacrifice our fostering relationships and social atmosphere on Sunday evenings. After all, that's what will build relationships leading to our goal."

Marcy again inquires of Tim's response. "You said unless something needed attention that evening. What could that be just by looking at the numbers?"

Tim purses his lips. "Very seldom would it be anything negative, in my thinking. But I would rather be prepared to address it on Sunday than wait two more days. Let's say for instance one of our Bible study classes normally runs twenty on Sunday morning and on this particular report it shows they had only eight in class. That is a huge drop and one that I would want to know about. Is there something we need to address that evening? Should we contact the teacher? It would be good for us to come together quickly to discuss it—briefly. Perhaps Roger knew that fifteen of the members of that class were away on a prayer retreat. It would sure ease my mind to know there was a logical response. However, if we found out something happened in the class that alienated fifteen people, we might need to take action right away and not wait until Tuesday."

Andy beams as with a revelation, "Sort of like when your engine light comes on in your car. You stop to have it checked at the next exit, instead of driving another seventy-five miles before checking it."

"Exactly. Sort of," Tim says jestingly at the way Andy began his reply. Tim continues, "Okay, Roger, will you look into having someone compile all of those and put them in our mailboxes on Sunday evening?"

Roger with a quick nod replies, "Yes, Linda Bishop tallies the number for our Sunday evening service. We can have her put them all together and photocopy them for us."

Tim looks at Marcy, Andy, and Roger to emphasize his next point. "You don't have to take a lot of time on Sunday evening. Just take a quick look at the numbers, and if you see anything out of the ordinary, check on it. If we all do it, we'll hopefully keep things from dropping through the cracks."

Greg regains oversight of the conversation. "Okay, that is one. Is that the only way you will measure followship?"

Roger reacts quickly. "I sure hope not. If numbers is the only thing we use, we're in trouble."

Following a few minutes of back-and-forth discussion of different ideas, Joe interjects, "In the business world, there is a thing called 'walk-around management.' Basically it is a leader or manager simply walking around the workplace, watching and listening to the workers as they are doing their job. You can really pick up some vital information observing what's going on and listening to the workforce. I think it would be good for you, the staff, and me as chair of the deacons to do some observation and listening, keyed in on followship, on a regular basis."

"That may be easier said than done," replies Roger. "On Sundays we're—or at least I am—so preoccupied with the worship that I probably miss half of what's going on around me."

Andy jumps in, "What? Oh sorry, I was preoccupied with something else." Then he busts out laughing. Everyone around the table joins him in laughter.

Roger recants, "Seriously, don't you all feel that way too?"

Tim comes to Roger's rescue. "I try to engage in conversation and what is going on around me. But I imagine what you are saying happens to all of us and more to you, Roger, than the rest of us. As the worship pastor, you have more details and more parts of the service on your mind and more people reporting to you. It's natural for you to be like that on Sunday morning." Tim pauses. Marcy, Andy, and Greg are nodding in agreement and in affirmation to Roger.

Tim continues, "I believe what Joe is talking about can reach beyond Sunday though. After the services, if not before, we are more relaxed. It is then that we can tune in to what others are saying and observe what is going on around us. And we can do it during the week."

Joe interjects. "It can be before, during, and after committee meetings. The same is true with mid-week activities. Anytime we're around church members—or attendees, visiting in their homes, eating with them at a restaurant. Wherever we are with them."

Tim is nodding and with an air of confidence suggests, "I like it. We're strolling the halls, trolling for information. Why don't we call it strolling trolling." He laughs. "I'm just kidding. What should we call it?"

Joe shrugs and says, "Why not call it 'walk around'? Here's what I saw in my walk around."

Everyone nods and makes different positive facial or hand gestures as to say what Roger verbalizes, "Why not."

Tim adds, "Walk around it is."

Greg, nodding with affirmation, declares, "Okay, you have followship as one of your driving gauges. You are going to on a weekly basis review numbers for regular activities and special events with a quick review on Sunday evening and as a team in your staff meeting on Tuesday morning. At that time, you will be seeking to make any necessary or helpful adjustments toward reaching your goal, your OG. In addition, you will each employ a walk-around attitude. Whenever you are around church people, you will listen and observe what is being said and done that can be applied to enhance your work toward your overarching goal. In other words, how are the words being said, the conversations being carried, and the actions of members moving toward engaging themselves and others in growing discipleship. Am I right? Is this what you are agreeing to?" He waits for a verbal agreement from each person.

"Let's move to your second driving gauge: *weekly questions and praying together*. What questions are you going to ask along the journey to ensure you don't get off track and to keep the pace needed to reach your goal?"

Andy raises his hand. "Are we talking about questions we are going to ask every week?"

Marcy interjects, "I thought that's what we were talking about: questions that we can ask every week any time along the journey." Susan looks at Marcy and nods in agreement, confirming this is what their discussion was about for this topic.

Tim concurs. "I think so. I believe we need a set of questions that we can ask each other every week or any time during the week—questions we ask of ourselves."

Greg inquires of Tim's response, "So, are you wanting a specific set of questions to ask each other?"

Tim nods. "Yes. I think we need two to three questions we can ask each other about the progress of the OG and about our own accountability. I am not saying those are the only questions to ask, but we need that built-in accountability and confirmation that we are on the right path." Looking at Greg, he adds, "Don't you agree?"

Greg tips his head, turns his hand about thirty-five degrees, both signs of affirmation, and says, "Yes I do. I wanted to be clear before we moved on." Looking around the table, Greg poses the next question. "What are two questions you could each answer every week to substantiate your conscientiousness and obligation to accomplishing the OG?"

Andy smiles and says, "Wow, That's a lot of big words in one sentence."

Greg, with an almost sheepish look on his face says, "Yes, I guess it was. Sorry about that."

Roger chimes in with a grin, "Sorry? No, I'm impressed. No need to be sorry."

Greg attempts to clarify his quest. "I agree with Pastor Tim that we all need accountability. I call it friendly accountability, and you all are the leaders and the ones to hold each other accountable. You are not going to beat each other up, but encourage one another and work together. To do this, I believe it is best if you come up with two or three questions that you will each be willing to answer at any time along the journey. And weekly is a good start." (Debrief: *Friendly Accountability*)

Tim once again comes to the rescue. "I think two questions we could ask each week are: 1) What specific thing have you seen in your ministry this week that demonstrates we are moving toward our goal, or that we are not? And 2) What have you done specifically this week to move us toward our OG?" Tim's two questions were so straightforward there was no discussion about them. There may still have been a little uneasiness about the accountability issue, but that is a natural response, even if everyone agreed. But the two questions posed were simple enough.

However, Joe does have an alternative. "Instead of the second question, Pastor, are you open to a self-assignment?"

Tim displays a puzzled look for everyone to see. "I'm not sure I understand what you mean, Joe. Can you explain?" All eyes and attention focus on Joe.

"Sure," Joe replies with confidence. "Instead of asking each other, 'What have you done this week?' why not set two or three weekly goals and report how you did on those?"

Now Roger has the puzzled look on his face as he asks, "What's the difference?"

Joe expounds, "You're not being asked the question each week. You set your own goals and you report on them every week." Joe points to the board where the four driving gauges are listed. Then he continues his explanation. "Your—ah, I mean, our—fourth gauge is to make personal visits. What if we each agree to make two personal visits each week? At report time in the staff meeting we could each take a minute to state if we made those two visits and the outcome. Instead of preparing something to answer the question 'what have you done,' you come prepared with the set criteria. It's easy to calculate. It does not take time to calculate or come up with an answer. I'm not part of the staff, but I'm happy to include myself, so you don't think I'm putting more on you. I'm willing to make the commitment. I'll make two visits each week."

"I like it," states Greg. "What else could you include in that report?" The thought processes kick into gear again. Marcy, Roger, and Joe all look at the board while contemplating the question as if to find an answer as Joe did with the visits.

All of a sudden Andy blurts out, "The walk around! We can tell how many visits we made and what we observed and heard during our walk arounds the previous week."

Greg is nodding with that half smile of his and says, "Exactly." Looking at Tim, Greg asks, "You already have the two-minute report incorporated into your staff meeting, right?"

Tim nods, and he and Roger simultaneously reply, "Yes."

Greg continues, "For the next seven months, this could be your two-minute report." Everyone is nodding in agreement. Greg adds, "You do not have to limit it to those two things. You need to discuss other possibilities as well. But for now let's look at the second part of this gauge, praying weekly as a staff. This is very important and needs to be a non-negotiable. Whatever you set to do, you need to do it every week. But this one, if there is anything that you hold on to and not let slip, it is this one. If you do not keep the prayer focus, then you might as well scrap it all. You'll be attempting it in your own power. So what is this prayer time together as a staff going to look like?"

One of Greg's aims at a retreat or meeting like this is to not leave anything on the table. He doesn't want any part of the process addressed lightly or swept away, especially the spiritual side of implementation. His theory: if a topic is passed over or lightly addressed at the retreat, it will have little significance in the implementation process. Therefore, he wants to ensure every aspect is covered appropriately.

Tim addresses the matter first. "I believe the appropriate thing would be to begin our meeting with the two-minute report, giving everyone time to express their findings for the week. Then, anything coming out of the two-minute report that needs to be addressed, we discuss it and immediately take the matter to God in prayer. In our prayer time, we can ask for God's guidance to the right decision. Following our prayer time, we can further discuss the adjustment or decision we believe God is leading us to." Tim pauses and with his eyes is seeking agreement or rebuttal from his staff.

With no disagreement, he moves on. "I believe we also need to spend time each week in prayer for God's direction in the upcoming week or weeks, moving forward toward our goal, our OG and fulfilling the Great Commission. We do not want to get sidetracked from our ultimate goal—the Great Commission—to focus only on getting x number of families involved."

Marcy interjects, "Correction, engaged, not involved. We want them engaged."

She smiles, letting Tim knows she understands what he meant and agrees with him. Tim replies, "You're right, Marcy. We want them engaged, not just involved. I guess we also need to watch our terminology. Still, we don't want to lose focus on God's directive of the Great Commission."

Looking at Tim, Roger poses a question. "Could that be a question we ask ourselves—as a team—every week? 'How are we fulfilling the Great Commission with our activities this week?' Not the week prior, but the week ahead."

Tim, his voice revealing a little embarrassment concedes, "We should be doing this already. And I take full responsibility for not leading us as a team this way."

Greg asks, "Okay, do you want that to be one of your questions for your driving gauges each week?" The team members are all looking at Greg as if seeking his approval that this should be one of the driving gauges. Recognizing the look from the team members Greg continues, "It is not my decision to make. It is yours." He pauses, "You should ask yourself the question; does it fit the criteria of a driving gauge?" He waits for a response.

Roger replies, "Yes. It is something we can see at a glance, any time during the journey, and it can be adjusted immediately."

Andy picks up Roger's line of thought. "We do not have to go through a lot of research. It either is or it is not fulfilling the Great Commission. You make the adjustments needed right then and there."

Greg inquires of everyone, "Do you all agree?" Heads nod around the table. Greg continues, "Then what is your decision? Is this one of the questions you will ask yourself each week?" There is a little hesitation this time, but all do nod in agreement after looking around the table to one another. (Debrief: *Leading by Questions*)

Turning to his left, Greg states, "Good, then we'll write that one down, Susan, as a driving gauge question: 'How are we fulfilling the Great Commission with our activities this week?'"

Greg leads the team in a similar discussion for the final two driving gauges. At the close of the session, the team has settled on how they will use the four driving gauges to interpret progress and process of moving toward accomplishing their overarching goal. For *Manifestations of Core Values and Fulfilling the Great Commission*, the team decided to ask each week, "What manifestations have we seen this week that give viable evidence that Calvert City Community Church is Great Commission driven?" Their hope is these will be openly visible and that the team will unearth some manifestations through their walk-arounds.

For their driving gauge of *Personal Visits,* the team decides to take two approaches. One will be staff visits. Each staff member and Joe (as chairman of deacons) have committed to make at least two personal visits each week, either in homes or sharing a meal or coffee with church members or prospective members. The intent of these visits is to build relationships, to encourage members in deeper engagement in service to God, and to lead people to faith in Jesus Christ. The second approach is to lead, train, and encourage other leaders in the church to do likewise. (**Debrief:** *Personal Visits*)

At the end of the discussion, Pastor Tim throws out the question, "Can you imagine if the six of us and only six other people accept this challenge and make two visits per week, what God could do? That's twenty-four visits, twenty-four personal face-to-face contacts each week, twenty-four people's lives we are impacting, saying we care about you. Twenty-four, that's something a church our size should be experiencing routinely. What can God do?"

DEBRIEF

FRIENDLY ACCOUNTABILITY

While many of us do not like the idea of being held accountable, God created within each one of us this need for accountability. The reason we shy away from or despise being held accountable is the negative connotation it holds for us in society today. Being held accountable goes against our desire to be independent. However, building friendly accountability into our personal life and ministry can bring a whole new level of trust and accomplishment to your team, no matter what size team you are on. In our story, the team members will set their own level of accountability. In this particular scenario, they will each set the goal of how many visits they believe they can make each week, while being fair to the team and their own ministry responsibilities and personal life.

Friendly accountability is that which does not hold a threat over someone but helps that person with encouragement to move forward, making progress toward his or her goal and responsibilities. Friendly accountability motivates a person toward the accomplishment of his or her objectives in a very positive and caring manner. Learn more about friendly accountability and try it with your team, at work, at church, even with your family.

One place where we see Jesus building in friendly accountability is John chapter 15. In verses five through eight, He uses the comparison of a vine and its branches to illustrate our connection to Him. Then in verses fourteen through sixteen, He uses these statements: *"You are My friends if you do what I command you."* And *"You did not choose Me, but I chose you. I appointed you that you should go out and produce fruit and that your fruit should remain, so that whatever you ask the Father in My name, He will give you."* Throughout the gospels and in other passages in the New Testament, Jesus encourages us in friendly accountability, each time noting He is with us through all.

LEADING BY QUESTIONS

Notice Greg did not give his opinion or answer the question, "Do you want that to be one of your questions for your driving gauges each week?" Instead he led the team to come to a right conclusion. How did he do this? Greg led them to come to the conclusion by formulating the right question. *"You should ask yourself the question, does it fit the criteria of a driving gauge?"* This question forces the team members to each consider the criteria for a driving gauge and connecting those thoughts to the destination, the Great Commission. Once they answered the first question, this is how a driving gauge works, their thought processes led them to recognize the connection to the overarching goal (OG) and their ultimate destination, fulfilling the Great Commission.

With this information in mind, the team is ready to answer the next question, which was the first question: *"Is this one of the questions you will ask yourself each week?"* While this question asks "will you," due to the thought process revelation and Pastor Tim's statement earlier, "We should be doing this already," the team sees this not as a "will you" but a "we must" imperative.

We have many examples in the gospel accounts of Jesus leading by questions, not the least of which is found in the final chapter of the gospel of John. From His first question in verse five to the last in verse 23, Jesus is leading and preparing His disciples for the future in one of His last appearances with them on earth.

PERSONAL VISITS

There is no stronger, more compelling impact on any human being than a personal face-to-face visit. While people today like to say otherwise, it just is not true. What is true is we have become a closed-in society. We do not even have to know or speak to our neighbors if we so desire. However, God created within each one of us an innate desire to have relationships. He created us to have a relationship with Him, and He created us to share relationships with one another. With today's technology, it is easy to communicate with one another by phone, text, social media, e-mail, and on and on.

Perhaps each one of those has its place in society, and each does some good. However, nothing will ever replace the encouragement, warmth, and affection as a personal face-to-face visit. Time and time again, we hear people who interact through video and audio media with family members in other states or around the world saying, "It's not like having them here, but it is the next best thing." In your ministry, do not settle for the "next best thing." Reactivate the personal, face-to-face, interactive visit; in homes, coffee shops, restaurants, parks, and any place you can. There is no replacement.

Jesus was all about personal visits. While there was at least one occasion where Jesus did not go when invited (for a healing), His entire ministry was about being in front of people—face-to-face contact—teaching, healing, instructing, and enjoying His friends and companions. It was not only a Sunday morning happening. Should we not be about the same ministry, ways, and means as our Lord and Savior?

Chapter 11

Putting the Pieces Together

When the team had finished establishing their driving gauges, all agreed it was time for a break. Following the break, the team came together for their next and final session of the day.

Greg, standing at the front of the room, begins the session with a question, "Where do we go from here?" He pauses, looks around the table, before asking a second related question. "What should be our next step?"

The young, energetic student minister, Andy, enthusiastically interjects, "Let's do it!"

Greg nods in acceptance of Andy's enthusiasm as he inquires, "Is there something we should do before we jump in and 'just do it'?"

Roger and Susan at the same time reply with one word, "Pray."

Everyone nods in agreement and Andy adds, "Yes, certainly let's pray. But I'm ready. We've got a plan. Let's get out there and do it. We don't need this to sit on a shelf. That's what I meant. God is going to do something great. I know it."

Greg smiles and says, "I like your enthusiasm, zeal, and confidence in God. We need more of that in our churches today. However, there are still some things we need to do first." Greg pauses to allow his listeners to absorb what he has just stated. The statement he has just made provokes a question in each person's head. It is a question that engages the higher-order thought processes once again. Greg's statement is this, "However, there are still some things we need to do first." The response this statement provokes is, "What things?" Greg is actually using a statement to actively pursue a question not verbalized. (**Debrief:** *Statements That Promote Higher-Order Thinking*)

Allowing a few seconds for those thought processes to engage, Greg continues, "We have looked at and discussed quite a few different things today, wouldn't you agree?" Everyone nods. "We looked at different phases of taking a journey, and we've translated those into your journey as a church, correct?" Again he pauses to get a nod of affirmation from everyone. "Do you believe it would be beneficial for us to put all those pieces together before we leave here today?"

Everyone nods and Roger interjects, "Of course, you must make sure you've got everything you need for the journey before you jump in the car and take off." Heads tilt and smiles come across the faces of Roger's colleagues at the mental picture he just painted.

Greg, now sitting down, admits, "Yes, another good analogy, Roger. In this session I want us to put it all together—gather everything for the journey, so to speak. Then we will close the day with a time of prayer—an extended time of prayer." Directing his next question to everyone, Greg asks, "If we left here right now, could you thoroughly explain what we've accomplished today to your ministry leaders and those to whom you are responsible for in ministry? Each one of you will need to do this in the next two to three weeks." He pauses. "Do you think you could?"

It does not take long for Tim to respond, "Probably not. Not thoroughly. If we all sat down together, we might be able to get close. But I doubt we could do it justice at this point."

Greg adds, "Right, and you will not have each other there at all sessions when you are talking about this."

Marcy jumps in, "Couldn't we have a couple of meetings to bring as many people into this as possible?"

Susan adds, "Like town hall meetings?"

"Yes," Marcy agrees.

Roger adds to the line of thinking, "We could have a meeting of deacons and other ministry leaders, then Bible study leaders, and after those a church-wide meeting. That way we'd be rolling it out, but not in one shotgun blast."

Greg, lightly tapping his pen on the table responds, "You can and you certainly need to discuss how you want to 'roll this out' to the congregation. But if you are not sure you can 'do it justice,' referring to Tim's previous comment, wouldn't it be beneficial to first put the pieces together and formulate a plan?" No one speaks right away as they understand what Greg is asking of them and realize they are not yet ready to clearly explain this to others in the church.

Following a seemingly long pause, Tim admits, "Yes, we need to understand it and see how all these pieces fit together."

Greg stands and steps back to the white board. Picking up a marker to use as a pointer, he says, "When we began this morning, we said [pointing to the drawing of the church] this is where we are at today. This is your church." Moving to the opposite end of the board, he points to the letters GC. "We also said that our ultimate destination is to fulfill the Great Commission, right? We need to understand that we are fulfilling the Great Commission as we go along the journey. Yet it is our ultimate destination. We are never to leave that journey, do you agree?" Everyone nods in agreement.

Walking back to the left side of the board, his right hand follows the arched line between the church and the letters GC. "This, we said, is the journey we are on to arrive at our ultimate destination. If our journey is to go from Richmond, Virginia to Los Angeles, California, we cannot make that trip in one day. Therefore, we need to do what?"

Roger replies, "We need to break it down into segments; segments we can drive in one day's time."

Greg nods. "Correct, and how does that apply to your church?"

Joe is ready with the answer. "We need to set an overarching goal to work toward in a shorter, specific time frame. In our case, the next seven months."

Greg responds, "Good. Can you state that overarching goal for us?" His question is not directed at anyone in particular.

Andy attempts to quote the overarching goal. "To go from twenty-nine families to forty by the end of the year."

Tim makes a noise similar to a game show buzzer disqualifying an answer.

"What?" questions Andy. "That's what we said, right, twenty-nine to forty?"

Tim replies to Andy's inquiry. "Your numbers are right. But your statement does not reflect our overarching goal, does it?" Tim scans the room as he closes his remark, which is a statement question. (**Debrief:** *Using Statement Questions*)

Marcy, who has been studying her notes, interjects, "*To move from twenty-nine families actively involved to forty families actively engaged in ministry and discipleship by the end of the year.*"

Andy is quick to retort, "That's what I said, isn't it?"

Tim is smiling. "Does anyone see the difference in Andy's and Marcy's statements?"

Following a brief pause, Roger states, "Yes. Marcy read hers off of her notes. Andy tried to quote it from memory. Andy should get points for trying to memorize it."

Marcy playfully hits Roger on the forearm for insinuating that she cheated by looking at her notes. Greg rejoins the conversation. "I have to agree with Tim. Andy's statement included the word *go*. While *go* works in the Great Commission, it might give wrong connotations to someone who has not been in these meetings today. Wording is important as you convey the message to everyone else. In fact it could be crucial."

Andy, wanting some semblance of vindication asks, "So what is the proper wording?"

Greg turns to his left. "Susan, can you give us the proper terminology as we worked it out and wrote it earlier today?"

Susan flips a page on her notepad and says, "Marcy had it right. It is, *'To move from twenty-nine families actively involved to forty families actively engaged in ministry and discipleship by the end of the year.'*"

Greg picks his train of thought back up. "The words *move* and *go* convey two different messages. And notice it does not say we are moving families. That could be misconstrued as we are forcing or coercing people. It says we are moving from twenty-nine to forty. Were there other differences between the two statements?"

This time Joe responds. "Andy did not include the words *involved* and *engaged*. I think that is critical wording."

Roger adds, "We certainly spent enough time on it this morning. It should be important."

Joe looks to Andy, "Nothing personal, Andy."

To which Andy jokingly responds, "No, that's okay. We can call this 'pick on Andy' session." Everyone enjoys a quick chuckle.

Tim joins the banter. "That's right. Andy just said 'go from twenty-nine to forty families.' That's a big difference from moving from twenty-nine families involved to forty engaged. That was a big part of our discussion this morning. Can the rest of you see the difference?"

Marcy states, "Yes, I do now. But I didn't realize how important it might be to get the wording right."

Tim adds, "I'm not sure anyone of us did. And if Greg had not asked the question, we might have gone back to the church and messed up our whole process."

Roger, Marcy, and Joe are nodding in agreement. Tim looks at Andy. "Do you see the difference, Andy? You just happened to be the first one to answer, but anyone of us could have said it similarly. So thank you for the learning experience for each of us."

Greg adds, "Yes, you simply paraphrased the OG. And we now see paraphrasing the OG can convey the wrong message. Better now, in this room, than giving a misinterpreted message to your congregation." (Debrief: *Leading to Build Up*)

Greg, ready to move the group forward, continues, "Okay, we have our current status, where we are. We know our ultimate destination, to fulfill the Great Commission. And we have our overarching goal for the next seven months. What do we need next?" As he surveys the six seated around the table, some are looking at their notes and some look to the board and flip chart.

Following about a seven-to-eight second silence, Joe declares, "Destination indicators."

Greg nods in agreement and asks, "Yes, and what are our destination indicators, the ones you know will be along your journey?"

Marcy is the first to respond. "Vacation Bible School is one of the first where we will be able to see how many families are involved and maybe engaged."

Andy immediately follows with, "Back to school. How many families will we see engaged when school starts in August."

Susan looks from her notepad to Greg and adds, "Our harvest festival and high attendance day in October."

Roger sums up the last two months saying, "All of our holiday activities and events for Thanksgiving and Christmas."

Greg glances at Tim then back to the others with a smile and a nod and says, "Very good. And what are some of the mile markers you can use in conjunction with these other points of interest to help you measure progress on your journey?"

This time Roger speaks first. "Attendance and giving; some of the normal things we count and keep track of."

Tim interjects, "And of course baptisms and people coming to faith in God and entering into a personal relationship with Christ."

With a slight twist of the head, Greg responds, "Very good. I think you all have the right idea." He pauses, giving everyone a time to take in what has been said and settle their minds before asking the next question. "You know your destination for the next seven months and what to look for along the way. What are you going to use to get there?"

Roger speaks first. "We use our ministries as our vehicle to get to the destination, but we must keep watch on our driving gauges."

Andy speaks up immediately. "Driving gauges. Asking the right questions every week in our staff meeting, and walking around—"

Roger interrupts, "Intentionally walking around to observe who is engaged and who needs to be."

Joe enters the discussion. "Personal visits. Each one of us will be making two personal visits each week and helping train and encourage others to do the same."

Greg is pleased as he asks, "Anything else?"

Tim says, "Yes. Prayer—praying together and leading our church in prayer through training, special prayer emphases, and seasons of prayer."

Greg states, "I'm impressed. Very good. What will you do with the information gained from these driving gauges?"

Roger sits up in his chair and begins, "What adjustments we need to make; a slight turn here, a sharp turn there."

Andy joins in, "Whether we need to slow down or to speed up."

Marcy can't resist and laughingly states, "For you, Andy, the speed up may not be a problem, but getting you to slow down may be our challenge."

Everyone laughs as Andy nods in agreement and says, "That may be true. I'm excited and ready to go."

Greg, who has enjoyed the fun along with the others, looks at Andy and says, "Boy, they really have been picking at you this hour, haven't they?"

Andy nods as Marcy replies. "Yes, but it is because we love him and his enthusiasm. It keeps the rest of us on our toes and eager."

Moving back to the subject at hand, Greg inquires, "Does this all fit together into a strategic plan for you?"

Everyone is nodding. Tim, Roger, and Susan simultaneously exclaim, "Absolutely." Andy and Joe nod and say yes.

Marcy states, "Putting this together this last session has been very helpful. It really became clear to me how it all works together."

"Good," says Greg, "Are you ready to put it together for the rest of us?" Marcy quickly looks down at her notepad, realizing Greg is wanting someone to walk through the process in front of the rest of the team. She is not ready to do that.

Greg looks around the table, expanding his opportunity to the others. "Who wants to give it a try? The others are here to help you if you stumble." Hesitation and silence pervade the room as everyone contemplates their own notes.

Andy looks to the front of the room and says, "I will." With that he gets out of his chair and steps to the front of the room. Picking up a dry erase marker to use as his pointer (following Greg's earlier example), Andy begins extrapolating the ideas of the process as he best remembers them. The others aid and assist him when he gets stuck or forgets something. No one is condescending or harassing to Andy. They realize they are all in this together. They are truly working as a team.

When Andy finishes, everyone gives him a round of applause for his effort. Pastor Tim suggests it is a good idea for all the ministerial staff to follow Andy's lead in walking through the presentation. Tim goes next, followed by Roger and Marcy. Joe invites himself to the activity and makes his presentation of the strategy as well. When asked if she'd like to try, Susan declines, stating she will just keep notes and support the others. Everyone enjoys another laugh, and Greg commends the group for their work and the effort of presenting the process and strategy.

The team takes a short break then comes back together for a time of prayer before leaving for the day. The prayer time begins with each one praying for the person to his or her immediate left. After all have verbalized a prayer for the person to his or her left, the prayer time turns to the elements of the strategic plan. Each person accepts a particular element of the plan, and they pray in order of the process. Greg begins praying for the current state of the church and its willingness to follow God openly. Susan then prays for the ultimate destination, fulfilling the Great Commission and that the team and church never lose sight of this God-given commission. Roger follows, praying for the overarching goal and God's intent for the church in reaching the goal in the next seven months. Andy prays for the destination indicators and the team's ability to read and understand the church's progress at each point of the journey. Marcy and Joe each take part of the driving gauges and the staff's decision ability and leading the church in making needed adjustments. Pastor Tim closes the prayer session putting it all together and praying for his staff and committed leaders.

Forty-five minutes after the prayer time began, the team gets up emotionally drained and spiritually charged from the prayer time and a mentally exhausting day that they are excited about—excited about what God has led them to accomplish in one day and the possibilities of what God could do in the next seven months. Now it is time to go start this next leg of the journey, the turn-around journey for Calvert City Community Church.

DEBRIEF

STATEMENTS THAT PROMOTE HIGHER-ORDER THINKING

Another way to promote higher-order thought processes is to use properly phrased statements at the appropriate time. Within the first sixty seconds of speaking to another person or group of people, your listener's attention will drift from your speech at least twice. You are the same. When listening to someone else, you will drift away briefly from what is being said. This drifting is not from outside distractions. Rather it is due to memory focus. As a speaker, teacher, or leader shares, our minds have a tendency to pick up on certain words or phrases and we begin thinking about an event or experience in our own personal lives. In most cases, the listener will quickly pull himself back into the current discussion.

We should remember that learning builds upon learning, and as we speak, the new material is being processed and attached to something similar in our listener's memory bank. This is what creates the learning experience and causes new information to be added into our memory bank. Since it is happening to our listeners every time we speak, why not take advantage of this natural occurrence and use it to produce learning experiences that produce results.

Learning to use this type of statement can be vital to your team remembering and carrying out the details of the project ahead. Planning and using this type of statement requires discipline on the speaker's part. Like a question, if you issue a thought-provoking statement, be certain to allow time for your listeners to process the information. These can be great discussion starters and can bring out great and creative ideas and enthusiasm from your team members. A good leader knows it is not only a good practice but vital in the learning process to not give all the answers but to lead your people in discovering answers for themselves. Jesus used this type of statement in various places, including John 14:2 and 4.

USING STATEMENT QUESTIONS

I love using statement questions. They are a great resource for the leader and teacher. Basically a statement question is formed by taking any statement and turning it into a question, isn't it? That was a statement question, by the way, wasn't it? And that makes two, can't you see? The last three sentences you've read, are they statements or questions? Yes, they are both. Statement questions can be used to bring facts into a conversation while setting the listener's higher-order thought processes into exploration mode.

Here are examples of statement questions possibly used in church. If you are in a budget planning meeting and some want to raise the budget and others do not, you might exercise this statement question. "We did reach our budget this year, did we not?" The statement is "we did reach our budget this year." The question, "did we not?" petitions each person in the room to contemplate the fact. This is a springboard for the higher-order thought processes allowing listeners to think of future possibilities. Follow-up questions can further the thought processes and discussion. A second example would be, "According to Acts 1:8, our first priority of missions is right here in our own community, isn't it?" While this statement question does not always require a lot of in-depth thinking, it does spur the thought processes and sets your listeners up for follow-up questions of how to reach the community.

Matthew 18 is one chapter in the New Testament that demonstrates Jesus using this type of question. *"Shouldn't you have had mercy on your fellow servant just as I had on you?"* (verse 33 NIV). Also in verse 12 NIV, *"If a man owns a hundred sheep and one of them wanders away, will he not leave the ninety-nine on the hills and go to look for the one that wandered off?"* Statement questions can be fun, especially when teaching others to use them. They can also be vital tools in your leadership toolbox. For more information on learning to use statement questions and cautions in using them, see chapter four of *Teaching That Bears Fruit*.[10]

LEADING TO BUILD UP

Successful leadership has various elements and practices. One of those is promoting positive behavior in others. To promote positive behavior in others, one must first understand and possess a positive behavior. One particular practice in promoting positive behavior is to at all times seek out and commend others and not to shun or forsake, especially in a learning situation. There are many people who will not attempt to try anything outside of their comfort zone. True learning, however, does not take place in the comfort zone.

When someone makes an attempt, as Andy did in this situation, you do not condemn them for not giving the correct or expected answer. Instead, you correct and praise him for the positive. In this scenario, Tim and Greg commended Andy for being the one willing to attempt something new. Yes, there was some teasing and joking with Andy, even from Andy himself, but the bottom line was Tim and Greg were not going to let this be a negative experience for Andy. They both asserted credit to Andy for 1) being the one of the group willing to step out and 2) leading in a learning experience for everyone on the team.

There are times in leadership for correction of a team member. However, always correct in private, not in public. Remember this, when there is praise to be given, praise in public; when correction is necessary, correct in private. If you want to build a successful, forward-moving team, do not allow your team members to be negatively impacted without encouragement. Always find something to use as a "build up," a positive outcome even from the negative or awkward experience. It will provide encouragement and give you a closer team member.

Chapter 12

Implementation

Pastor Tim has wasted no time following the retreat. The next morning he holds meetings with Andy and Roger regarding their respective ministries and how to implement the strategies right away. Andy and Tim discuss possible opportunities for the students of the church to bring in new students representing new families. Each week, as Andy goes on personal visits, he is going to attempt to take at least two students with him. His reasoning is to train those with him in making personal visits and to bring encouragement among peers for the students being visited. Andy will also challenge his student volunteer workers and teachers to make personal visits as well as regular communication through other means with the students. Andy's words are, "While some of this is already ongoing, we want to be intentional about reaching out to and communicating with our students. If we're going to see lives changed, we must."

Andy also commits to Tim to introduce more ministry and missions opportunities for the students to be involved and engaged. His commitment is to have at least one ministry or missions activity each month. Tim commends Andy on his intent, commenting, "The students will learn much more and remember it when they are engaged in a missions effort. We are all that way. It is inbred in us. Application is at the root of all learning." The two discuss other areas and ways to strengthen the student ministry. While the student ministry is not "weak," it is about to take off with a new paradigm.

Roger's meeting with Tim is about incorporating into worship the explanation, exhortation, and significance of the overarching goal for the next seven months. As Tim says several times in this meeting and in the meetings to come, "We must keep the OG in front of our people, all the time." This will take place through various means: Pastor Tim will preach about it and attempt to, as God leads, share something about it in each week's main message. They will incorporate the OG in the special prayer time and in other prayers throughout the service. Roger agrees to pray about and research worship music and scripture that expresses God's desire for the church and the members need to be engaged.

In addition, at least once each month, Roger, with Tim's approval, will attempt to incorporate a different worshipful resource for engaging in the overarching goal. These include testimonies, videos, dramatic skits, and interviews of members and recipients of ministry from the church. Adding to this, Roger's plans are to equip the choirs and praise team in carrying out the vision for accomplishing the OG, not only with special holiday music performances, but every week leading up to their weekend worship settings.

Roger and Tim later that day sat down with Susan to plan written publications for the rest of the year and how to incorporate the OG in every publication and media in the church's ministry base: the weekend program, on the screen in the services, the monthly newsletter, the church's website and Facebook page, and even the church bulletin boards. This alone will be a major undertaking, and Susan has already been thinking through and experimenting with the printed materials that are part of her duties. Roger will begin that evening speaking with the different church volunteers who are responsible for the website and social media and the media screens for worship services.

Not wanting time to slip away, Pastor Tim meets with Marcy that same evening following the mid-week activities to begin discussing her role in this with the children and family ministries of the church. They discuss similar avenues as with Andy and the student ministry and how Marcy could carry those out with her volunteers in the children's ministries. They also discuss the events that come under Marcy's purview: Vacation Bible School, a back-to-school event, and the Fall Family Festival. Marcy's plans are to strategically work with her volunteer leaders and children's ministry council to not only produce successful events but to engage more members and regular attendees in the planning and operations of each event. In addition, the team will strategize how to engage more families from outside the church in attendance to the events and to move some of those families into involvement, which would lead to engagement in the ongoing ministries of the church.

Pastor Tim conducts meetings on Thursday with Darryl Larson, the small group Bible study/Sunday school director, and Joe Greer, the chairman of deacons at 4Cs. Tim and Joe's discussion deals with how the two of them will roll this out to the deacons at their meeting the following Sunday. What will be the responsibility of the deacons? Tim and Joe lay out some ideas but agree not to take their ideas to the deacons as "this is what must be done." Rather, Joe will share the heart of the team for reaching people and the overarching goal, to focus on families for the next seven months. Tim then will lead the deacons in a discussion allowing them to discover ways they can best serve and be effective servant leaders for the church. They close the meeting with prayer and confidence that the deacons will be on board leading with this focus.

Joe also sits in the meeting with Darryl Larson. Pastor Tim and Joe explain the process the team has undertaken following their assessment of the current reality at 4Cs and the need for a strategic plan to move the church forward. Following their explanation, Tim states, "Darryl, you know I am a firm believer in our Bible study small groups that meet on Sunday, and I believe we can and should use this largest organization in the church to propel this endeavor. I need your input on how we can best get our people not only involved but engaged in not only reaching our goal, but in making this part of who we are. It should be what we do on an ongoing basis, long after this year is past."

"I'm all in," says Darryl. "It might be the one thing we've been looking for to really cement our classes into real thriving missionary units."

"Good," replies Tim, "What ideas do you have?"

Darryl purses his lips for a second then says, "Well, following our face-to-face summit, we've said one thing we need is monthly equipping meetings for our teachers and other leaders. We have the first one scheduled for one week from this Sunday. I think this will be a great place to begin."

Tim and Joe both nod in agreement and Joe acknowledges, "We were thinking the same thing."

Tim, still nodding, says, "We'll need to work together to do this, and I've asked Joe to help since he was at the retreat with the staff. I'll have all the staff there as well."

With a slight twist of the head right to left in an upward motion, Darryl replies, "Great, what do you need me to do?"

Tim doesn't hesitate. "First, get the word out. Let's try to get ninety percent of our workers to that meeting; more if possible. We all need to be involved in getting the word out. You and I can meet next week, and we'll come up with first steps, so you can be ready to implement those through the classes right away." Tim pauses, allowing Darryl time to process this information and acknowledge his understanding. Darryl gives a nod, and Tim continues. "We will lead those in attendance to make some of the decisions of how to engage the class members, but we will need to guide them as this is all new to them."

The conversation continues for another fifteen minutes. The three men pray together for discernment in how to address the leaders and for the ability to guide the meeting to bring glory to God while bringing excitement and exhilaration to the members of Calvert City Community Church.

At home that evening, Tim is helping his wife, Leigh Ann, in the kitchen after supper. "I may go into the office for a few hours tomorrow. I need to think through this. Who am I leaving out?"

No one knows a pastor like his wife, and Leigh Ann is in tune with her husband's ever-functioning mind. "Slow down," Leigh Ann says with a laugh. "Tomorrow is your day off. I know you spend a few hours in the office on many of your Fridays off, but you need to remember, this is a marathon, not a sprint." Tim looks up. He respects his wife's response.

Leigh Ann continues, "You've been at this all week, late nights Tuesday, Wednesday, and today. You need a break. You need a day to let your mind settle—a day to rest, mentally, physically, and spiritually." Tim is nodding. He knows the importance of taking time regularly to rest and let God restore his depleted energy. But it is hard for him. Tim is a thinker and a doer.

"Besides," says Leigh Ann, "From what you've told me, I think you've had meetings with just about every leader in the church this week, preparing for this. Who could you possibly have left out?"

They both smile, and Tim answers, "I don't know, but even if I'm here tomorrow, I don't know if I can stop thinking about it and processing it."

Leigh Ann is nodding with tightened lips, "I know. I know how you are. But we'll just have to try. We talked about maybe going to the park with the kids tomorrow. Let's do that. That will keep you occupied for a while."

Tim nods in agreement and adds, "I guess I could get out and do some yard work in the morning before we go to the park."

Leigh Ann now has a different smile on her face. "That's what I like to hear. Isn't it you who is always telling others, 'You will not be good to anyone if you work yourself into burnout'? Take your own advice. You're in this for the long haul. And you've got seven months to go. You don't need to try to get it all done in four days."

Tim crosses the kitchen to give his wife a big hug. "Thanks for being such a good listener and advisor. I love you and appreciate how you care for me."

The next Tuesday, the staff comes together for their first staff meeting since the retreat. Greg is also in the room, along with Joe, who has adjusted his work schedule to attend. Andy begins with a devotion, reading from Psalm 23 and commenting about the need to wait on the Lord and be patient, not trying to run too fast or run ahead of God. As he finishes, he states, "This one hit me hard. I know I like to run headlong, and there are times I need to slow down and allow the Shepherd to have me sit down and digest what He is doing."

Tim shakes his head left to right and reveals, "Me too. It's not only you, Andy. My wife had to share that same thought with me again Thursday evening." Solemn looks appear on everyone's face. "It's hard sometimes to slow down. You know what God has laid in front of you and you want to go, go, go. But that's the fast road to burnout." Tim pauses for a second. Then to lighten the air he remarks, "In fact, I thought Leigh Ann may have talked to you and had you prepare that devotion for me."

Everyone enjoys a brief laugh before Andy replies, "No, it was for me as much as you, Pastor."

Roger adds, "I think God intended it for all of us. We all need to be reminded from time to time."

Andy then leads the group in prayer relating to their ministry service and the topic and truth found in the scripture and devotion he has shared.

Tim looks around the table with a fresh look of encouragement and says, "Okay, two-minute reports. Marcy, start us off this morning. What have you been doing since the retreat, and what do we need to know of your schedule this coming week?"

Marcy straightens up in her chair. "Last week after I met with Pastor Tim, I began speaking with my key workers, asking them to pray about their own involvement and engagement in the lives of our children and their families. I am happy to say I have spoken with all seven of our key children's leaders, and they are on board and considering ways to implement our strategy through the children's ministries of the church. Also, I have two appointments set to visit with families tonight, and I'm taking Jean Price with me."

Marcy pauses for just a second, and that is all Roger needs to jump in. "Overachiever," he says jokingly. Everyone smiles, including Marcy, as Roger does tend to tease her from time to time about her detail and efficiency.

Marcy continues, "Also, on the way home Wednesday evening, I began thinking about the conversation Greg had with our waitress, Jenn, a couple weeks ago. I don't know why, but for some reason God put her on my mind. I have not had a chance yet, but I want to go back to the restaurant and talk with her. I want to help. I want to see what we—our children's and family ministry—can do to minister to her family. I've already talked with Jean and Maggie about a possible parents' night out. So that's all in the works. Pray for Jenn and that I can follow God's lead in helping her."

Tim is smiling and nodding with a pleased look of affirmation as he verbalizes, "Thank you. You've been busy, and I appreciate that. You might be an overachiever [referring to Roger's quip], but that's one of the qualities that makes you so good at what you do." Tim turns to his left, "Susan, how about you. What have you been up to, and what do we need to know?"

Susan finishes writing something in her meeting notes before speaking. "Well, Pastor Tim, Roger and I met Wednesday and began looking at our print and promotional publications. We are going to go through a program makeover. I have started looking at ideas of how we can include the OG in our weekend program and our newsletter. Roger and I will be working with others to perhaps come up with a logo or something that is recognizable and can be used in all our media publications. It will be a few weeks, but you may start seeing some changes pretty soon." Jokingly Susan adds, "So when people see changes, you all be ready to take those arrows for me."

Tim inquires, "Very good. Anything else?"

Susan looks at her notes. "Not on the OG or the retreat, but I need all of your newsletter information by Thursday at noon." Everyone is aware of the deadline, but a little reminder never hurts.

Tim picks up the conversation again. "Okay, Andy, why don't you go next."

"Sure," replies Andy. "Pastor and I met Wednesday as well. Like Marcy, I will be going to all our student ministry leaders and speaking to them. Unlike Marcy, I have not gotten around to them all yet." Marcy smiles at Andy, and everyone smiles along. "I have spoken to Robert and Amy, my two key leaders. I am planning to have a meeting with all the others this coming Sunday instead of one-on-one meetings. I may follow up with more one-on-one, but I want to share the OG and the process with them as a team. I'll be working on that meeting this week, so if anyone wants to help, feel free to volunteer."

Tim, cautious of a scheduling dilemma, inquires, "What time Sunday are you planning to have this meeting?"

Andy is ready with a response. "After the small groups meeting and the other Sunday evening activities." Sensing a little unrest from Tim, Andy continues, "We've already made them aware of it. In fact I gave them two choices. That's the time they all preferred."

Tim nods in acceptance. "Okay, good. I'm glad you were thinking ahead and being proactive. I just didn't want it interfering with the small groups meeting. In fact I'll get with you. If they all attend the small groups meeting, we'll be explaining the entire process there. It may save you some time in your meeting."

Andy lets out a big sigh of relief. "Whew! Good. That's the volunteering I was asking for. Oh, one more thing. I have two in-home visits lined up this week, and I'm taking two of our students with me on each visit."

Tim has a confident look of satisfaction on his face. "Great. You guys are doing great. Joe, do you want to go next?" Joe tells of his meetings with the pastor and Darryl and a couple of informal conversations he has had, as well as the deacons meeting held the previous Sunday evening. "The deacons are all on board. They were excited and I believe rejuvenated at having a new direction and vision." Joe finishes and turning to his left, turns the floor over to Roger. Roger takes his turn to inform the staff of his engagement the past week and his schedule for the week in progress.

Tim is the last to share. He shares with the others of his various meetings the previous week and planned meetings this coming week to help implement this OG and the process to accomplish it. Then he changes course. "That's my two-minute report, and I believe I did it in less than sixty seconds," he says tongue in cheek. "Now I want to talk to you about something that has been bothering me this weekend and I began working on yesterday." He shares about his conversation with his wife, Leigh Ann, on Thursday evening, then says, "It was good for me to take that break." (**Debrief:** *Break for Reset*) "I needed it for what I believe God revealed to me Sunday morning sitting in the worship service before I spoke to the congregation." All eyes and minds are on Tim. Someone could walk into the room, drop a book, and not one of the team would notice.

Tim continues, "I think we've missed a main point, and we need to reconsider our process." Looks of despair now overtake almost everyone in the room—all but Greg. Although Greg's higher-order thought processes have kicked in with Tim's last statement. He pulls his thought patterns back to hear what Tim has to say.

"We've talked about involvement and engagement, and while these are good and I believe we are on the right track, I believe we need to improve our strategy and our wording a little." While there seems to be a little relief on some faces, everyone is waiting in eager anticipation for what Tim is about to say. "It seems to me all of our talk of being involved and engaged was about in the church or the church ministries. Should we not be driving towards engagement in the community?" Tim stops and waits for rebuttal.

Roger is the first to speak. "But that's what we have been talking about, getting people engaged in the community through Bible study groups and other ministry efforts and activities we offer."

With one nod of his head, Tim agrees, "That's exactly my point. We're setting our goal on getting people engaged in church ministry efforts. Those are all good and likely will produce some growth—spiritually and numerically. But is that our ultimate goal?" This time silence overtakes the room as everyone's higher-order thought processes kick in.

Following about fifteen seconds of silence, Andy speaks up, "Well, if you are talking about our ultimate destination, it's to make disciples. Are we not doing that with our process?"

Tim simply responds, "Are we?" addressing the entire group. Tension builds in the room, not anger or friction, but apprehension concerning their approach. Each one begins to contemplate, *"What are we missing?"*

Another ten seconds of silence passes before Joe speaks to the question. "The first part of the Great Commission says to 'Go and make disciples.'" He placed an emphasis on the words *go* and *make*. "We may be giving them opportunities to go, and to go as a group, to be involved in the activities and events that the church sponsors. But are we truly providing relational building gospel opportunities?" Tim glances over to Greg. It is obvious by the expression on Greg's face that he is aware of what Tim is leading the team to understand and hopefully correct. They both realize Joe is on the right track.

Roger, looking at Joe, shakes his head, not in defiance, but in needing clarity. "Can you help me out here? I'm not sure I follow you."

Marcy with a puzzled look interjects, "Yes, me too, please."

Joe nods in acceptance of the inquiry. "We know that we are to go, and as we go through life we are to share the gospel, right?" He looks at Roger and Marcy for affirmation. They both nod in agreement. "To do that, we must be among the people in society, don't you agree?" Tim and Greg both smile, realizing Joe is using coaching skills with the other team members.

Joe looks around the table to acquire a nod from everyone. "Instead of a series of one-time events where we have an occasion to meet others, shouldn't we be placing an emphasis on relationship building between our congregation and the outside world?"

Marcy quizzically states, "But we do. We always encourage them to be involved and build relationships."

Tim pulls everyone's attention back to the front of the room, continuing the discussion. "We may say it and hope to encourage them, but are we compelling them, giving them a reason to want to build other outside relationships?"

Marcy, with a puzzled look, shares her thoughts, "I don't get it. How are we supposed to compel them? We cannot force them into relationships."

"You are right," voices Tim. "So what can we do? What is within our power to help our members move towards building relationships outside the church?"

Roger jumps at the open invitation. "Train them—we need to provide training on how to build relationships that may result in sharing the faith, the gospel."

Andy is shaking his head. "I don't disagree with you, Roger. Pastor Tim is often reminding us that whatever we do, we are called to equip our people, our congregation. And I agree, but there must be more than training."

Greg is nodding in affirmation of Andy's statement and states, "I agree with Andy. Our churches have had training courses, programs, and events for years. Unfortunately they become just that: courses, programs, and events. Training by itself is not an indicator of potential growth in any area. Tim's question was, 'What can you do, what is within your power to help church members move towards building relationships outside the church?'"

Marcy asks, "Can we pray about it—I mean right now?"

Somewhat surprised, but glad that she brought it up, Tim says, "Certainly!" With that Tim bows his head and begins praying aloud. "Father God, You are God Almighty. You know our thoughts. You know our discussion. Open our minds as Your leadership team for 4Cs. Open our minds and hearts to greater ways to be Your hands and feet, Your mouthpiece and voice to all those in our circle of influence. And help us in this room to be the leaders You have called us to be for this, Your body of believers at 4Cs...."

When he closed his prayer, Joe immediately spoke up. "What we want them to do, we must first lead by example. They must see, hear, and know that each one of us are already involved in building relationships with unchurched people. Training and equipping them is one thing, but practical demonstration is a whole new dimension." (**Debrief:** *Lead by Example*)

Roger looks at Joe with a little surprise, "Wow! Where did that come from?"

Joe tilts his head to the right slightly and says, "While Tim was praying, it just unfolded. He asked, 'open our minds as your leadership'—"

Tim interjects, "And He did. He revealed it to you." Looking around the room, Tim inquires, "What do you all think?"

Marcy affably states, "Well, it's kind of hard to argue with Joe's statement coming right after prayer. If that isn't a God answer, I don't know what is."

Susan, pulling away from her notepad, says, "Yes Joe, Thanks for listening to God through that prayer and not being hesitant when the prayer was over. I'd call that a God moment."

After a moment of private reflection, Tim leads the team in a discussion, asking each one where they are building or could build relationships outside the church with unchurched people. Each person in the room comes up with a possible person or situation; a hobby or leisure activity where they can look for God's guidance in fostering at least one new relationship and to pray for God's guidance in moving those relationships toward a gospel presentation. Andy is involved in the local high school sports teams and commits to intentionally begin building relationships with some of the coaches and players. Marcy commits to do the same with some of the PTA parents at her children's elementary school. Roger plays tennis for exercise and frequents a local music store and agrees to start building relationships there. Joe, Tim, and Susan commit to similar avenues with neighbors and acquaintances through their hobbies.

Marcy, with a big smile and renewed enthusiasm in her voice exclaims, "Wow isn't God great? I didn't see that one coming. Did anyone? Yet God led us to a key leading endeavor."

DEBRIEF

BREAK FOR RESET

Perhaps it is built into leaders, this drive to go, go, go, billowing at a project like a fast-moving monorail train that has no brake for slowing or stopping. Do not get me wrong, I believe we need to keep the train moving forward and build momentum along the way. However, I believe successful leaders understand—or have someone to help them understand—that in most planning and decision-making projects there comes a time when a break is needed. One principle I have learned, practiced, and try to pass on to others is that of *Break for Reset*. We can get so involved and wrapped up in looking at a project or situation from a particular vantage point that we can miss opportunities for greater potential.

I have on occasion advised my wife to stop working on a particular project if she was becoming frustrated and could not come to a solution. And no, I'm not speaking of having difficulty with her husband. One instance in particular was balancing a bank statement that had her frustrated and ready to throw in the proverbial towel. My advice was to set it aside and come back to the bank statement later or even the next day. When she came back to it, she found the resolution and was finished within five minutes. I have done the same on many occasions—walk away and come back later—take a break and come back refreshed with a renewed and reset mind. Following a break for rest and coming back with a clear mind, it is amazing how clearly and simple an answer comes to some situations that seemed nearly impossible earlier.

My wife and I were laying hardwood flooring in our bedroom. This was not our first time as we had laid hardwood flooring in two other rooms in this particular house and in a large room in a previous house. We had been working all day on this room and came to the last strip of flooring. Each piece needed to be cut lengthwise and fitted not only along the edge of the wall but around the base of two French doors as well. I ran into a situation—how to get the last two pieces in as one would need to be locked into place and tapped under the door trim. I thought and thought, measured and contemplated. It was a real dilemma. It was late and we were both tired.

We decided to stop for the night and finish the final two pieces the next day. I took a short break then began cleaning up the room while my wife was in another part of the house. About a half hour later, I was almost finished picking up and putting things away when the solution to my situation came to me clear as the ringing of a bell.

The longer I stayed in the mode of trying to solve the issue, the more tunneled in thought I became. But once I stopped thinking about it and gave my mind a needed rest, the answer came, without me trying to process it. To give her the credit, my wife had recommended a similar solution forty-five minutes earlier that evening. But I was so tunneled in my own thought processes that her suggestion did not register.

Taking a break to reset can be invaluable to your leadership, your family, and your own mental and emotional stability. We all need to step away from situations and projects to clear our minds and reset our thinking processes. When something has you so wrapped up, take a break. Do not think about that project for a period of time. Force yourself, if you need to, to put it out of your mind and think on something more pleasant and enjoyable. Your mind cannot reset if you continue to think about the issue needing resolution. Take a break and reset for a clear perspective. And if you need to, make sure someone in your circle of influence has your permission to tell you to break and reset as Leigh Ann did for her husband, Tim, in our story.

LEAD BY EXAMPLE

Leading by example is not a new concept. It has been around for centuries and beyond. It was certainly a major concept of Jesus' ministry and leadership. He is our supreme model for leading by example. In the church and the corporate business world, however, we sometimes fall short. We lead by example for particular areas of responsibility. But those portions that we are uncomfortable with or that we feel we do not have time for are often dropped. And in most of those areas, we do not realize that we are not leading by example as we should. Actually, in those times, we are leading by example, but not the right example. What gets recognized gets emphasized, and what gets emphasized gets recognized. Bottom line, if we want others to do it, we must be willing to get right in the trenches with our team and congregation, not pushing them, but rather leading the charge.

Chapter 13

Small Group
Bible Study Leaders

The following week, Andy walks into the Bible study leadership team meeting at exactly 4:00. Roger looks at Andy with a friendly smile and says, "Right on time. Now we can start the meeting."

Andy smiles back and replies, "Glad I could oblige and be your starter clock." Those who know of Andy's habit of exact promptness smile and laugh.

As Sunday school director for the church, Darryl Larson begins the meeting welcoming everyone and leading the group in prayer for the organizational structure and spiritual well-being of the leaders and the members. "Our Father, God in heaven, we come to You at this hour asking for Your blessing and indulgence as we begin a new day, a new era in our church's largest organization, our Bible study ministry. May it in the future be fruitful in introducing people to Christ and growing people into maturing disciples for You. Lead us to develop a structure that demonstrates caring, compassion, and loving unity for all You bring our way, that no one would fall through the cracks. Today, as we look at how we as leaders can guide our classes in fulfilling the overarching goal of our church for the next seven months, show us Your ways, that we can lead in them. Thank You for the vision and goals You have led our pastor, staff, and others to develop for us. May we, each person in this room, be found faithful in carrying out Your plan and Your intentions for this church and the surrounding community, and guide us to lead our classes in the same as we grow together as maturing disciples of Jesus Christ...."

When he has finished his prayer, Darryl introduces the plans for the meeting. "This afternoon we are going to look at how we can lead the Bible study classes, our Sunday school and classes that meet at other times through the week, to fulfill the Great Commission through an overarching goal that has been set by the pastor and leadership of the church. You have heard the pastor mention the overarching goal in his last two weekend messages. He is going to come and share with you the overarching goal and the plans that we need as Bible study leaders to work toward this goal. We're calling it the OG, short for overarching goal. Then he will lead us in a discussion on how you believe God would lead you to implement this through your class." With that being said, Darryl turns to where Tim is seated and says, "Pastor, come and lead us."

Tim steps to the front of the group and begins, "Thank you, Darryl, and thank all of you for being here this Sunday afternoon. I am excited about what God is doing and what I believe He wants to do through this church. As you know, earlier this spring we brought Mike Davis, one of our denominational leaders, in to help us conduct a vigorous face-to-face summit with reality. This was an intense look at the brutal facts of where we are as a church. We looked at the decline of certain areas in our church over the past ten years, finances, membership, and attendance. Not only these areas, but also we realized through this vigorous summit process that we have not been engaging the community as the church once did." Tim pauses, allowing this information to sink in. Most heard about this when the report was given and in other meetings and sermons since concluding the summit.

Tim continues, "We also realized that as a church we have failed in other areas as a New Testament church. Some of those we imposed on ourselves intentionally. As resources grew smaller, we intentionally pulled back on certain ministry efforts. In other areas we slipped away from what we should be doing without even knowing. And let me remind you, it does not matter who was here or not here in that ten-year timeframe. You and I are here now, and we are to take full responsibility and move this church forward to be all that God created it to be. Are you ready to do that with me?" Tim begins at the left side if the room and slowly turns his head from left to right, expecting and anticipating heads to nod in approval. Most everyone responds in the affirmative with a nod of the head or eye contact and body language. It is evident those in the room are absorbing what their pastor has just stated. Some have a look on their face as though they just realized for the first time that they are a leader in this aspect of the church. It is as though they thought of themselves as only a teacher of weekly Bible studies, not as a leader of God's people.

Following this pause of self-reflection, Pastor Tim explains the process that the staff and chairman of deacons have been involved in, seeking God's will for the church. "It has involved scripture, prayer, and many hours of meetings over the past month before we were ready to unveil it. It is still a work in progress, and we need your input today. Let me explain." Tim takes the next ten minutes extrapolating all the parts of the strategic plan, beginning with drawing on the left side of a white board the little church and on the right end of the board the word *mission* with the letters GC directly under that word. He continues drawing on the board and explaining the process, just as Greg had done at the retreat, divulging the destination indicators and driving gauges as well.

When he is finished, Tim asks the staff for further input. Roger speaks to the group about the Great Commission being God's directive to the church and the overarching goal being what the church believes they need to do to move them along the journey, in this case for the next seven months. Andy shares with the group of his excitement and desire to "really make this happen" as God intends. Marcy speaks to the moments of spiritual renewal for her in particular as the staff has walked through the past two months and this discovery process.

After they have shared, Tim once again addresses the group. "One thing we realized last week is this must be bathed in prayer and the spiritual side must be accentuated. We also must strive to use this as a permeating of the culture around us." Tim turns to a small table he had set up prior to the meeting. On the table sits a clear pitcher of water and a glass bowl. Inside the bowl is a kitchen towel. Standing at the table, Tim begins to share, "This bowl represents the world. Inside the bowl is our sphere of influence." He holds up the towel for everyone to see, then places it back in the bowl. It is the community around us. Not only around the church, but where we live, work, and play. You have influence with everyone you meet and spend time with. This towel represents your circle of influence." Tim pauses, looking around the room to ensure everyone is following his analogy.

"This pitcher of water represents us, 4Cs church. The pitcher might be our building. But the water is us, each one of us individually and corporately." Tim states as he holds the pitcher up. Then he begins to pour water from the pitcher into the bowl. "When we pour ourselves into our circle of influence, something happens." After pouring about half the pitcher into the bowl, Tim picks up the towel and says, "The towel still looks the same. It has not changed colors, it has not changed shape."

Water is running out of the towel into the bowl as Tim continues. "It is still a towel. What has changed?"

From the second row, Bob Simons, a teacher with the student ministry, calls out, "It's wet."

From the other side of the room Susan Hawkins claims, "It's saturated!"

"The change is that the water has permeated the towel." Tim, holding the towel in his right hand over the bowl, begins squeezing the towel at various places. "No matter where I squeeze, I find water. The water has permeated the towel." Tim places the towel back in the bowl. Wiping his hands dry on another towel, he continues, "As a church, I believe we have failed to permeate the culture around us. Could this be the reason we have seen decline in the past ten years, because we have not been the penetrating, permeating water God has called us to be in our circles of influence?" (Debrief: *Object Lessons*)

Something has permeated the room. It is silence as everyone ponders what they have just experienced. Following a long fifteen seconds of silence, Tim breaks the quietness. "This afternoon we need your help. You are the leaders of our Bible study ministry; as Darryl said in his opening prayer, this is the largest organization in our church. We need you need to realize this is the largest organization of our church and capitalize on it. I want to ask you to get in groups of four and discuss as the largest ministry of 4Cs—how are we going to lead our people to not only be involved in ministry to the people around us, not only to engage in ministry, but to permeate our circles of influence with God's love and Christian living." Tim pauses, then adds, "We as a staff have our goals and our priorities. But each and every ministry must do the same. The deacons met last Sunday and set some objectives to move toward our OG. Now it is your turn. I want you to take five minutes and come up with one or two ideas as a group."

As the groups begin, Tim interrupts, "Remember, we are not looking at good things we can do to give our people something else for their already busy schedule. We are looking for ideas on how to engage our people and ourselves in permeating the community for God."

Miss Sue Bellamy, who teaches the eldest ladies class in the church, raises her hand, "My ladies are all in their eighties and nineties and we don't get out much. Some don't even drive any longer. I just don't know what we can do. I think it's a great thing to do and as a church we should, but we're just too old and we don't get around."

Tim gives a nod of understanding. "Thank you, Miss Sue. I understand, and you are right. Your class might be limited in what they can do, and their circles of influence may be not as large as the rest of us, but your ladies are such prayer warriors, we need them involved." Motioning with his right arm to the group sitting with Miss Sue, Tim says, "You as a group have a great challenge in helping find things that Miss Sue's class can be involved in through this time in our church." With that everyone turns back to their group and discussions begin.

Notice in the previous exchange with Miss Bellamy, Pastor Tim did not rebuke, belittle, or degrade her in any way. He did not tell her she was wrong (which many pastors and leaders might have done). Rather, he agreed with her sentiment—to a degree—then encouraged her and those around her, issuing a challenge in a loving manner not only to Miss Bellamy but also to the group to assist her.

When the five minutes was complete, Tim called for the groups to come back together as one. He then went around the room asking each of the small groups to give one of their ideas. As the team spokesperson called out and explained the team concept and reasoning, Tim wrote the idea on a large flip chart pad. After each group had given one idea, he started over and asked each group for a second idea. Some ideas were duplicates. Some ideas were grouped together to make one, while others were discarded after discussion if they did not meet criteria of reaching outside the church to fulfill the Great Commission. When the discussion drew to a close, there were seven ideas on the pad.

Tim turned from the pad to the leaders. Placing the cap on his writing marker, he asked, "Can we do these?" He paused, looking around the room. Receiving expressions of affirmation, he continued. "You came up with these, I did not. The staff did not. You did as leaders, and I commend you for that. I believe these are all doable. However, not all of these are doable by everyone. You do not need to try all seven. What I want you to do next is to get in groups by your teaching age divisions—preschool and children's class leaders over here [extending his right arm to his right], the student class leaders over here with Andy [to the left], young and median adult leaders here [motioning to front center of the room], and senior adult class leaders, well since you are seated together already, right where you are.

"Here is your assignment. I want you to work together to choose two of these you will promote and use in your class or department. Remember the illustration. You want to help your class members to permeate their circles of influence. You are working together as a group to help each other, but especially adult and student leaders, you must have a plan for your particular class. We will help you implement these, but I want you to choose what you believe fits best for your class and discuss why in your group. You have fifteen minutes."

Following ten minutes of discussion, Pastor Tim and Darryl visit with each group individually, handing out index cards, two per person, with the following instructions. "Each person should write the two ideas you are going to take back to your class on these cards. Write your name, your class name if you have one, or the age parameters for your class. Under that, write the two ideas you have chosen to take back to your class."

When the fifteen minutes has passed, he gives more time for people to finish writing on the index cards. "When you finish, your two cards should look identical. You are to write the same thing on each card. Once you have finished and both cards are complete, hand one of the cards to Darryl. He will collect them. Keep one for yourself to use as you pray through and focus on leading your class in those two ways listed on your card." Darryl gets up and moves around the room as hands extend with one of the index cards.

While some are writing, Tim calls for volunteers to share what they have written and why they believe their class will accept this challenge and run with it. Four people share. Sharon is the last of the four to speak. "Our class has a bowling team. We joined the bowling league four years ago as a way to fellowship and show our Christian walk to others. However, tonight I realized we are using it more for our fellowship than building relationships and permeating our circle of influence. I am going home and talk with Allen, my husband, to suggest that instead of having a team of class members that we join different teams in the league. Allen and I join one, Bill and Beverly join another, and Phil if he desires can join a third team. This way we can build relationships with those team members not in church and hopefully permeate parts of the league as our circle of influence." Heads are nodding around the room. It is evident everyone is appreciative of Sharon's comments. There appear to be some "aha" moments going on as well. Sharon goes on to say, "My prayer is that leading by example we can encourage others in our class to do likewise in their circle of influence.

Adam Duxworth, a man in his mid-fifties, speaks up, "I golf as do several others in our class—and in the church for that matter. We could do likewise. I know several men in my class play on a Friday afternoon league. I am going to encourage them to do the same. Thanks, Sharon, for the idea. And as for me, I don't play in the league, but I can begin to play with certain individuals not in church with the purpose of living in front of them and leading them to understand why I am who I am."

Jay Duncan, a man in his early thirties, chimes in, "Adam, I've been thinking about how we as golfers can host a golf clinic or maybe several over the course of the year. Make them weekend, Friday evening, Saturday clinics working on specific parts of the game. Not only to work on the golf game, but to introduce people to Christ. Let's talk afterwards."

Pastor Tim, with a smile as broad as his face and emotion welling up inside, clears his throat to say, "Thank you all," nodding toward Jay, Adam, Sharon, and the others. "You have blessed my heart." Addressing everyone, he says, "God is so great, and I am so blessed to serve alongside you. In just the little time we have spent together this afternoon discussing this, you have come up with some brilliant ways to permeate your circles of influence. May this enthusiasm spread throughout our Sunday school and our church!"

With excitement in his voice, Johnny Barker, who has been teaching a median adult class for five years, says, "I'm excited about this and encouraged. Thank you, Pastor and staff, for helping us see something and giving us an opportunity to lead like this. Today I realize this is more than church as usual. This is working as the early church did. We have forgotten that over the years. This has given me new life, new hope, and a new purpose for leading my class to truly fulfill the Great Commission." Several others around the room comment with a yes, amen, or "likewise," and heads are nodding throughout the room.

Tim thanks the teachers and leaders for their input and enthusiasm and states, "I think you have done a wonderful job today. However, if it stops here, we have done nothing but talk. We must carry this forward and hold each other accountable. And most of all, we must pray. I want us to spend the rest of our time in prayer. I am going to ask you to get back in your groups, peer teaching groups, and pray together. Then in time, I will ask Joe Greer, our chairman of deacons, to close us in prayer." Tim gives a few thoughts on how to pray and what to pray for about the process. The groups spend the next twenty minutes praying together before Joe closes the meeting in prayer and dismisses everyone. (**Debrief:** *Incorporating Others and Dispersing Prayer Challenges*)

DEBRIEF

OBJECT LESSONS

Object lessons are a great tool for leaders in part because they begin with the learner's context in mind. Jesus used many object lessons as recorded in the gospels, and there are many others throughout all of scripture. "By using object lessons, Jesus demonstrated that effective learning builds upon what the learner already knows."[11] When contemplating object lessons to be used in leading, consideration must be given to the relevancy of the object and its use to your listeners.

When an object is produced in a leadership environment, it should be an object everyone on the team can relate to and understand its use and purpose. In our story, Pastor Tim used a pitcher of water and a small towel. Everyone in the room knew the objects being displayed. Likewise, when Tim poured the water over the towel soaking it, everyone knew the changed condition of the towel, now fully saturated with water.

The second thing that must happen with an object lesson is the connection between the object lesson and the leadership truth or principle being conveyed. Having a good, fancy object lesson without a true and easily understandable connection to what you expect from your team members will only distract and perhaps confuse team members. Following every object lesson, illustration, and story should be a time of debriefing to assist your learners in full comprehension of the concept and truth. Personally, I like to lead the team through the debrief session as a discovery learning experience. In other words, I use questions to ascertain the level of understanding of the connection between the object lesson and the principle or truth by team members.

In our story Tim gave a brief explanation of the comparison between the object lesson and 4Cs church. Then he asked for help from the leaders. He then led them in a discussion to discover concepts of how, through the Bible study classes, they could use the analogy to impact the ministry of the church to the outside community.

Object lessons begin with something the listener already knows and allow, through demonstration, the listener to attach the new information to what is already embedded in his memory. Attaching new information to something already stored in our memory bank produces learning based upon something we already know. This is learning building upon learning. Object lessons provide lasting learning experiences.

INCORPORATING OTHERS AND DISPERSING PRAYER CHALLENGES

It is not enough to pray ourselves and to talk of praying. We must incorporate others into the ministry of prayer. Church leaders must teach their people to pray, equip them in prayerful manifestations, and incorporate them in prayer emphases for the church and the lost or unsaved as well as the hurting and those in need. Standing in the pulpit or sitting in a classroom and asking people to pray or reminding them to pray is not enough. However, in too many churches this is the extent of the prayer ministry.

There is great joy and much to be accomplished when we pray together. Praying of like-mind for the will of God will bring God's favor on our prayers and endeavors in ministry. Jesus knew the significance of prayer, and though He was God in human flesh, He took special time to pray and taught His followers to pray according to God's will. Are we not God's followers? Study prayer. Ask God to take your prayer life to a deeper level. Then lead your family and church to do the same.

Chapter 14

Hurdles

Over the next two weeks, similar meetings were held with other groups by various staff members explaining the journey from the OG to the driving gauges. Each ministry was asked and encouraged to determine what their part was on this leg of the journey to fulfill the Great Commission. Not all of the teams were as enthusiastic as others, and there were some difficulties and hurdles in implementing a few of the ideas and carrying out the initial desires for fulfilling this leg of the journey.

While in the small group Bible study leaders meeting a lot of ideas were made and there was no vocal pushback, when it came to implementing those ideas, not every class jumped at the opportunity.

On his way to the office the first Monday in July, Tim's cellphone buzzes. He recognizes the buzz tone as an indicator that someone has sent him a personal message on social media. Curious, when Tim pulls up to a red traffic light, he pulls his phone out to see who the message is from: Darryl Larson, his Bible studies director. He sets the phone down in one of the car's cup holders and proceeds to the church, only three minutes away.

Shutting the car's engine off in the church parking lot, Tim picks up his phone and opens the message to read it. "*Do you have time to meet with me today? I have a couple concerns I need your help with. Half hour tops. Darryl.*"

Tim walks into his office, greeting Susan as he walks by her desk, checks his schedule, and replies to Darryl Larson's social media message. "*10:30 or 3:00. Which is best for you? Tim.*" Tim thinks to himself, "*Social media has its advantages. That was quick, easy, and painless.*" Tim also knows that had Darryl contacted him with an e-mail or voice message, Tim might not have picked up or replied to the message for another hour or more. As that thought is running through his head, his phone buzzes again. He opens it to see this brief message from Darryl, *"10:30 thanks!"*

While Tim is pleased with the brevity and quick responses offered by using social media, his thoughts quickly turn to wonder what is so urgent for Darryl to need this meeting right away. After all he had not said anything yesterday, Sunday, when they were together. Did something happen during the Bible study hour or maybe after church? Were they facing a rebellion? Could it be something in Darryl's personal life? Was his business in trouble, losing his job maybe? Could he and Doris, his wife, be having trouble in their marriage? Tim tries to convince himself it has to be about the Bible study ministry at the church. Nevertheless, Tim automatically heads into prayer mode.

He gets down on his knees in front of the sofa in his office and begins praying out loud, "Lord, You know what is going on in Darryl's life. You know why he is troubled this morning and You know his concerns. Ease his mind even now as I speak to You. I do not know what it is that has him troubled this morning, but You do, O Lord. Give him comfort until we can speak and then allow us to come to a conclusion and point of restoration for whatever his concern is. Lord, if it is something going on in the church, give me wisdom and discernment. I am not a fixer, but You are. You have called me to lead this church, and if something is broken or needs to be addressed, lead me—lead us—to Your perfect solution...." Tim continues to pray for Darryl and Doris and their marriage and home life. He wants to cover all the bases.

After his time in prayer, Tim walks out to Susan's desk to advise her that he is expecting Darryl Larson at 10:30. He then returns to his office and proceeds with his regular Monday morning routine, reviewing Sunday's attendance and financial reports and looking through the guest cards that had been placed on his desk by the head usher for those who visited the church the day before. Returning the guest cards to Susan, Tim will now begin checking e-mails. Deleting some, passing others along to staff members and replying to the ones he needs to, Tim will spend thirty minutes each morning reviewing and replying to e-mail and phone messages. On Mondays, however, that thirty minutes can easily turn into an hour. Like social media, Tim appreciates e-mail. He is glad to be living in an age with quick communication. He often jokes about not having to depend on phone calls, personal visits, and the pony express for communication with one another.

Finishing up with his e-mail, Tim turns to the short stack of postal mail Susan has laid on his desk. Before he can read the first piece of mail, the intercom on his desk phone chimes. It is Susan: "Pastor, Darryl Larson is here for your 10:30 meeting."

Looking across the room at the mantel clock resting on a bookshelf, Tim realizes it is 10:27. *"Well, that's Monday morning for ya,"* he thought. Looking back at the phone, he replies to Susan, "Send him in. Thanks, Susan."

The door opens and in walks Darryl. At six feet three inches tall and about 240 pounds, Darryl can be a pretty imposing figure if he were not your friend. Tim has already risen from his chair behind the desk and moves toward the door to greet Darryl. The two men exchange hellos, and Tim motions for Darryl to sit in one of the chairs in front of the desk; Tim sits down beside him in the matching chair.

Tim shares with Darryl about the prayer time he had for Darryl after receiving his message earlier. "I'd like to begin this meeting with prayer as well."

Darryl nods, "Yes, always."

Tim offers a prayer for Darryl and the discussion they will engage in once again, asking for wisdom and discernment. Following the prayer, Tim looks over to Darryl. Their eyes meet as Tim states, "You mentioned in your message that you have a couple of concerns. Why don't we jump right in and you tell me what those are?"

"Well, maybe it's just one, but it's big enough to be two," Darryl begins. "In our Bible study leaders meeting last month, everyone seemed to be eager and ready to take this new direction. You'll remember they seemed excited and were not only listing what they could lead their classes to engage in, but they were also coming up with ideas for their own personal engagement." Pastor Tim is nodding in acknowledgement of what Darryl is referring to and is relieved that it was not trouble in Darryl's marriage. "Well, I just don't see much of it happening. I am concerned that it will all die out and our work and that meeting will be in vain." Darryl stops, waiting for Tim to speak and respond to his concern. Tim, however, does not respond. Instead he sits, eyes locked on Darryl's eyes, and continues nodding with a somewhat quizzical look on his face as if to say, "Yes, tell me more."

Following a moment of awkward silence, Darryl speaks again. "I don't know what to do. What are we going to do, Pastor? What should I do?" Though he could give Darryl a series of steps to undertake, Tim instead moves into coaching mode. (**Debrief:** *Coaching*)

"Darryl, we prayed and planned for that meeting and delivered a solid vision and strategy for the journey, did we not?"

"Yes, we did," replies Darryl.

"And as you said, they not only received that information, they also showed excitement, responded, and even wrote out steps they would take. You have a copy of those cards they wrote on, correct?"

"Yes, and I've been praying over them, but I just don't see anything happening."

As a smile comes across Tim's face, he asks, "Darryl, when was that meeting?"

Darryl looks a little puzzled. "*Surely the pastor has not forgotten that meeting.*" After all, they had just been talking about it for the last five minutes. "Two weeks ago. You remember, Sunday afternoon."

Tim is nodding. "Yes, I remember. Again, tell me how long ago?"

Darryl, still with the puzzled look, replies, "Two weeks ago yesterday."

"So they could not have shared it with their classes until last Sunday, correct?"

Darryl nods with a quiet yes.

Tim continues, "Is it possible we have not heard much back because they are still in discussion mode to determine how each class is going to undertake their challenge?"

Darryl nods eagerly. "Yes, I'm guessing, even hoping that is why. Still, I do not want this to fade away. I think it is the most positive initiative we've done through the Bible study groups in a long time. We can't let it die out."

"Okay, Darryl, you've been praying through those cards and the initiatives the teachers and leaders turned in. What else can you do to insure this does not fade—and I agree, we do not want to let it fade away."

Darryl thinks for a moment then replies to Pastor Tim's question: "Well, I've thought about asking each one of them how it is going, what their class has decided on, and when I can expect something in writing from their class."

That's good," Tim responds, "But I would ask you to think through it a little more. See if you can make it even more positive, affirming their initiatives, encouraging each one to send you regular updates instead of asking for or giving a mandate for an answer in writing. Do you understand the difference?"

Darryl, looking confident, responds, "Yes. I think so. Asking them for a deadline for something in writing can sound somewhat imposing."

"Correct," replies Tim. "People do not like to be told anything. And while you would be asking for a deadline and something in writing, it is an arresting statement. It almost comes across as a demand."

Darryl interjects, "I see."

Tim wants to reinforce this learning experience, so he continues. "While there are times when that approach is necessary, what do you believe with our volunteer leaders might be a better strategy? Think of what is of importance here. Is it getting something in writing or actually seeing action being taken and hearing of results?"

Darryl quickly answers, "Action!"

Tim shares a few more thoughts on how to encourage responses from the Bible study leaders, prompting them to stay on track with the initiatives, before Darryl thanks him and gets up to leave. Tim walks Darryl out the door and thanks him for his concern and desire to see the Bible study ministry become a more vibrant and essential part of the spiritual health of the church.

Pastor Tim heads back to his office to read through the remainder of the mail and return a couple of phone calls. At 11:45, the office phone chimes. "Pastor," it was Susan. "Bob and Terri Janes are here, ready for lunch." The Janes had been members of 4Cs for about twelve years and had seen the church go through some pretty rough times in that period. Bob was a deacon and helped out around the church with small construction and remodeling jobs. Bob was retired from the local fire department and recently semi-retired as a self-employed carpenter. Bob's wife, Terri, had worked outside the home for a few years but left the work force when her husband retired from the fire department. Terri taught Sunday school in the children's department and served on the church hospitality team, working in the kitchen for all church meals.

Pastor Tim enjoys going to lunch with the Janes. They will call about every two to three months and want to take the pastor to lunch. Tim enjoys the time with the Janes because he knows they love the Lord and support His work. There will certainly be questions from both Bob and Terri today at lunch about some of the innovations and changes in this "turn-around journey" the church has undertaken. But Pastor Tim is confident that Bob and Terri will be advocates and even cheerleaders for the journey. This lunch will not be like the one Tim had last week with another deacon, Frank Bottom, who invited Tim to lunch to school him why this "journey" was not a good idea. Frank's whole premise was that change is not good. *No, this lunch is going to be a very positive one,* Tim thinks to himself as he picks up his keys and heads out to meet the Janes.

Later that afternoon, Tim has a meeting with Roger, the worship pastor, and Susan, the church administrative assistant for an update on a new ministry to begin the next evening. A weekly visitation is to be implemented, something that has not been in place for more than a decade—and one that Frank Bottom had spoken in opposition to at lunch last week with Pastor Tim. Frank likes being at home evenings with his family and is not comfortable visiting in other people's homes.

The weekly visitation was implemented and accepted with enthusiasm by the staff and most other leaders in the church, other than Frank Bottom, realizing the benefits that regular, intentional visitation can have on the health of their church and ministry for God. With Vacation Bible School (VBS) only weeks away, the staff has made plans to begin the weekly visitation two weeks prior to VBS. This will give the staff two weeks to iron out the bugs, so to speak, and have the visitation ministry running smoothly by the time VBS follow up comes around in three weeks.

In the meeting, after some general information is given about the next evening's opening night of visitation, Tim turns to Susan and inquires, "Do we have a good number of prospective visits to be made?"

Susan nods, "I have pulled the guest cards from the past six weeks [guest cards turned in by people visiting the Sunday services], typed the information on visitation sheets, and am printing maps to go with each one. We have about nine families we can visit."

Tim looks a little puzzled. "Nine, that's all? That will not get us very far. If each team takes two, we only have enough for four teams. What if more people show up?"

Roger chimes in with a little sarcasm. "It would be nice to have more. But in reality, we might not have enough people to make up four teams on our first night. After all, we've only been promoting it for two Sundays. I don't mean to sound pessimistic, but—"

Tim interrupts, "You may be right, but we need to be prepared. The Sunday morning guests should always receive priority, but we need other avenues as well. Who else can we visit?"

Susan glances at Roger then back to Tim and suggests, "What about the Bible study class lists? We could put those out and let class leaders take their list to visit class members."

Tim is nodding. "Great idea, Susan. Each team could take a guest sheet and their list. Visit the guest first, and if you have time, visit someone on your class list."

Roger now eagerly jumps into the conversation. "Especially those we haven't seen in a while."

"Or prospects," Tim adds. "Each team could take at least one guest sheet and a class list. If we need to take more than one guest card, we can, to make sure they receive a contact. We certainly want to thank them for attending and see if there are needs we can meet as a church family." Tim pauses for a few seconds before asking, "Anything else?" Susan and Roger inform Tim of the set-up they have discussed for Tuesday evening visitation: how to log out the sheets, knowing who is going where, and how to retrieve the guest sheets with follow up. The three pray together for the visitation program, and each one returns to their office to continue the work of the day.

TWO WEEKS LATER

In the Tuesday staff meeting following Vacation Bible School, both excitement and concern is in the air. Joe, chairman of deacons, leads the team in a devotion and prayer time, then everyone gives their two-minute report. All the reports are mostly positive and encouraging, though Pastor Tim and Andy, Minister to Students, are the only two who have completed their two visits for the week. Tim feels the need to address this. "I realize last week was a very busy week. We all had more on our plate than usual. And I am excited about the seven older children who made professions of faith in the Lord last week. However, we have made a commitment to make two visits each week. Marcy, I know you have already followed up with two of those children and their mothers. In my opinion, since you did that following Vacation Bible School, you fulfilled your commitment, even if it was on our property. The visit does not have to be in the home, but if we are the church leaders and we make a commitment, we need to follow through with that commitment. Do you agree?"

The room is silent. The team realizes the accountability button has just been engaged. After a seemingly long ten seconds of silence, heads begin to nod around the table. Andy speaks up, "Vacation Bible School only comes once a year, but what can we do as a team to help encourage each other and keep our commitments with the larger than usual workload?" His question is not one of doubt or refute, rather it was a call for collective improvement.

Roger takes up the gauntlet. "I think we need to realize there are going to be weeks where we will not be able to keep those commitments."

The look on Tim's face gives evidence of what his next statement will be. "Then is it really a commitment? Are you not saying it is only a commitment as long as it fits comfortably in my schedule?"

"The pastor is right." It is Joe. "Our commitment is only as strong as our actions. If we don't follow through on a consistent basis, then we've not made a commitment but a convenience action. I made only one visit last week, and that was to a member in the hospital, so I am speaking to me as well as all of us. We're called to lead this church, and they'll not reach beyond our leadership."

Marcy joins the conversation. "I agree. We are leaders, and this is one thing we talked about and Greg spoke to us about at the retreat. We cannot allow the whirlwind, the busyness of church work and ministry pull us away from our commitment. Otherwise we will not accomplish our OG. I commit to all of you right here and now that I will do better and not let the whirlwind get to me. And I for one appreciate this accountability." Looking at Tim then back to each of the others, Marcy continues, "I need you all to remind me and encourage me. I need that friendly accountability." Greg, the team's strategy coach, takes particular notice to observe everyone around the table as Marcy finishes. The facial expressions and body language of everyone is in agreement with Marcy, as if they are saying, "the same for me." Everyone except Roger, that is; his body language is almost defiant. Roger tries to hide his displeasure and disagreement. However, it is somewhat obvious to everyone in the room and easily picked up by Greg. (**Debrief: *Body Language***)

Tim decides that the point has been made and enough time has been spent on the subject. Therefore he decides to move the discussion forward. "Well, I believe we will have enough tonight to keep us all busy fulfilling our commitment this week." Looking to his left, Tim asks, "Susan, what can you tell us about tonight?"

Susan looks at her notes and replies. "Well, it looks like we have about thirty visits we could make tonight. We have fourteen families from Vacation Bible School who do not have a church home, including those seven who made decisions for following God. We also had three first-time guests in the church services this weekend and two that we need to follow up on from last week. In addition to these, we have three families or couples who need a second visit. So you're right, Pastor, we have enough for this week and to make up for last week." Susan smiles as she looks at Pastor Tim, who is smiling as well. Actually, everyone around the table is smiling at Susan's advantageous report and her final comment.

DEBRIEF

COACHING

Professional coaching in the Christian world has become an increasing widely used form of leadership over the past decade. There are aspects to coaching that all leaders can learn and use to effectively guide people in growth, achievement, strategic planning, implementation, and fulfillment in Christ. One of the great benefits of coaching is guiding a person or group in discovery and effective implementation. In our story, Pastor Tim could have given a series of steps and possible solutions to Darryl's dilemma. Instead, Tim chose to coach Darryl in discovering the areas Darryl himself was gifted in and could carry through with. Notice it was Darryl, not Pastor Tim, who came up with the suggestions and ideas to implement. Coaching is a very effective tool in leading and growing people into self-sufficient leaders.

DEBRIEF

BODY LANGUAGE

The words you speak make up only 7 percent of your communication. This means 93 percent of what you communicate is delivered through your body language, eye contact, facial expressions, vocal tone and inflection. Every twist of the head, movement of the eyes, wrinkling of the brow and hand gesture is communicating to those around you. You will notice throughout our story various body movements and changes are noted. Each one adds to the verbal communication. A person's eye contact, voice inflection, and body language speaks greater volumes than words. Study body language and these other non-verbal communication nuances we all use and you will be able to lead your team more effectively.

Chapter 15

Fast-Forward

In the months that follow, Calvert City Community Church (4Cs) is experiencing joy-filled ministry. Yes, there have been ups and downs. There have been headaches and hurdles. But the staff and leadership team have pressed on toward the goal and have kept the church focused on the outward-purposed opportunities God is providing. Let's look in on a staff meeting the second Tuesday in September.

Following the devotion and prayer time, Tim states, "Okay, Marcy, start us this morning with your two-minute report." Marcy looks at her notes, then around the table. "Okay, we had a good day Sunday. All teachers were here in their room fifteen minutes prior to starting time. My team is good about that. Last week we followed up with three more families from the back to school event that we held three weeks ago. We had good visits, though none of those families made commitments to be here yet." She purses her lips and cocks her head to the left and in a very positive tone states, "However, Sunday, one of the families we visited two weeks ago was here, Mom Dad, and three kids, for the first time." Everyone around the table gets their first shot of adrenaline for the meeting. Roger, Joe, and Greg simultaneously said, "Great!" The others made similar comments and nodded with enthusiasm.

Marcy continues, "We have four more families that we have not visited from the back to school event. So hopefully we can see those this week. I know Andy has one of those scheduled, right?"

Andy nods towards Tim and says, "Yes, this evening."

Marcy resumes, "Last month's leaders meeting helped our preschool and children's teachers to obtain three more volunteers this week to help in preparing crafts and contacting parents. This is a big win as we needed them and we still could use two more." She pauses briefly then states, "Overall, I believe we are seeing motivated leaders and even our children are excited about bringing new friends with them. We had four children who brought a friend Sunday."

"That's good," says Susan and others around the table share similar words of encouragement.

Marcy adds, "The one thing I believe I have done this past week to move us toward our OG is encourage the teachers in pursuing volunteers and visiting families, which in turn helps us fulfill the Great Commission."

"Great," says Tim. "I know of a couple of other things you have done this past week as well to move us toward our OG." Tim does not reveal what those are but lets Marcy know that her labor and love for the ministry has not gone unnoticed. "Roger, What about you?"

Roger looks a little uneasy and straightens up in his chair as he begins, "Well, I didn't make any visits last week. I only had one scheduled and they had to cancel. Tuesday I was practicing with Janie and Lois, two college students, working on their duet for next Sunday, and we did not get finished in time for me to go out."

Andy jumps in with a question. "What are you doing to make sure you do not have a repeat of those circumstances this week? And how can I help you?" This is perhaps why Roger had that uneasy look when called upon. He knew he was going to be held accountable. Pastor Tim is pleased that Andy asked the accountability question. Tim has trained and encouraged his team to hold one another accountable. Instead of Pastor Tim questioning Roger, it is Andy who questions Roger, and he does it not in a demeaning way, but more in a way of offering assistance.

Roger looks down at his notepad then back to Andy. "I am not going to schedule anything that might conflict with going out on Tuesday to visit, and if I set an appointment, I am going to set more than one in case one has to cancel. I am also planning to visit a couple of former choir and praise team members on Saturday morning. So I'll make up for last week." He pauses as if waiting for approval. There is no verbal response, so Roger continues, "The multimedia team is working on a video with brief sound-bites of testimonies from people who attended the back to school event. It should be finished tomorrow evening to be used in Sunday's service." Looking to his left to Marcy, Roger states, "Twice on Sunday I heard two different people saying something about the back to school event and what a good job you and your team did. They are still talking about it three weeks later. That's good. That's an affirmation of one of our destination indicators."

Greg, who has been sitting silently, interjects, "That's one of your driving gauges for one of your destination indicators. Good job, Marcy, Andy, and everyone who was involved."

Following another pause, Roger claims, "What I did this week to move us toward our OG is to write notes of encouragement to four families who have not been real regular in attendance in the past year."

Andy asks, "What kind of encouragement?"

Roger, looking at Andy, replies, "Telling them we miss them and have a place for them and look forward to seeing them on Sunday. Two of them used to sing."

Andy is nodding and affirms, "I like that. A note of encouragement goes a long way. We sometimes have the students send cards like that to their classmates. I should probably do more of that myself."

The conversation moves around the table, each one giving their report and being held accountable by his or her peers when needed and encouraged by one another with their actions and reports. When all have shared, Tim turns to Susan and asks, "What can you tell us today? What are our other driving gauges telling us?"

Andy interrupts, "Wait, I have something else. I have heard from three of our students and two or three adults. They like and appreciate the devotions we are providing. Has anyone else heard any feedback?"

Roger nodding says, "Yes, I have heard three or four people comment on the devotions as well—all good comments, by the way."

Joe, chairman of deacons, chimes in, "Same here. I have heard several people speaking about them and wanting to make certain they get a copy each week. We may need to continue it on past the eight weeks scheduled."

Pastor Tim is nodding with affirmation. "I believe it is doing some good. People are reading and praying. They are taking it seriously. And I believe it is one reason we are seeing progress. People are praying in unison, and God is answering prayers. Thank you, Marcy. I believe that was your idea. I am glad we pursued it and glad you all have participated in writing them." With no further comments, Tim looks to Susan, giving her the go ahead to proceed.

Susan, looking at her notes, states, "Well, as Marcy said, we had the one new visiting family on Sunday, and we had another family of four, the Shepherds, back for the third time since the back to school event. This week they were in Bible study *and* worship—"

Roger jumps in, "And I heard Mrs. Shepherd sings. So I want to talk to her this week about getting involved in the music ministry." Nods of approval come from around the table.

Susan continues, "We also had two other first-time adult guests Sunday. One was from out of town, visiting family, and the other was a neighbor of Bob and Janice Jones." Flipping to another page on her notes, Susan gives the visitation and contact updates. "Last week we have recorded seven staff visits." Susan nods her head, acknowledging the visitation accomplishments of the staff and Joe. "In addition, we had nineteen people Tuesday night: thirteen went out on visits, four wrote cards to absentees, and two stayed in the nursery with the children. In all, we made fourteen visits and sent twenty cards out. In addition, Ima Joy and the seniors made six visits last week, and three others were turned in by Sunday school classes. That's twenty-one visits in all."

Tim, with a pleased look on his face, asks Susan, "And how many did we have this week last year?"

Glancing at her notes Susan reports, "Three."

As team coach, Greg takes the opportunity to interject. "That's what happens when you make a decision to be intentional, include your people, and do something for God. In May you made a decision, prayed, and refocused for God's direction. When you determine to step out and give God the lead, He will bless. From three to twenty-one—that's a 700 percent increase. That's something to celebrate." Looking at Tim, Greg continues, "You need to stand in front of your congregation this Sunday and let them know this is happening. Celebrate this—700 percent increase! And if I counted correctly, you had at least twelve guests." Heads are nodding. Tim is writing himself a note. Greg turns back to Susan and inquires, "What is your attendance compared to last year?"

Again looking at her notes, Susan reports, "Bible study is up twenty and worship is up thirty-one over last year."

With a really big smile on his face, Greg suggests, "See? Isn't God great?" Smiles cross the faces of everyone in the room.

Tim clears his throat and states, "It *is* great, and we do need to celebrate, but I want to go back to Marcy's report. There is something that should be troubling us in one thing Marcy reported." Focusing his gaze on Marcy, Tim continues, "Marcy, you stated that we still have four families who attended our back to school event that we have not yet visited. Does that trouble anyone besides me?" Tim pauses, takes time to slowly pan the room with his gaze and waits for someone, anyone to respond. That old familiar silence encompasses the room.

Roger, the worship minister, looks down at his notes, perhaps with a little guilt because he could have made at least one if not two of those visits. In fact, no one is looking up. All heads are down until Joe, the chairman of deacons, speaks up. "It has been over three weeks, and we have not made those visits. It doesn't appear that we have been real intentional about thanking them. It doesn't set well with people when it takes a month to get a response from something like this."

Andy adds, "It also doesn't look like we care about them. What if one of those families had a crisis or a need?"

Roger jumps in as if to defend the church's non-response. "But I don't think they were expecting a visit anyway, were they? Aren't we making the visits out of courtesy and thanking them for attending the back to school event?"

Joe and Andy both start to respond at the same time. Joe's voice carries as he responds to Roger. "That may be true, but it is not the attitude we want to convey to others, is it? 'We'll get to you if we get around to it'? We live in a world of instant communication. Three or four weeks is an eternity when it comes to conveying a message." Joe pauses and Marcy takes the opportunity to jump in.

"I don't like it, but I have to agree with you, Joe. I'm the one responsible for follow up. Sorry, I feel like I've let the team down. I should have done more, made sure we got someone out to see them." Greg is ready to interject, but waits momentarily to see if Pastor Tim will take the lead. Tim does.

"Marcy, what more could you have done?" The tone of Tim's question is inquisitive, not affirming. He wants Marcy to think of other avenues that could've been taken to avoid the situation. He allows Marcy time to ponder. The learning opportunity may be directed at Marcy, but everyone around the table contemplates possible solutions as well. After a brief time of silence, Marcy responds, "I don't know, really. I can't force people to go out to visit."

Andy jumps into the conversation and offers a suggestion, posing it as a question to everyone. "Isn't it just as much our responsibility as Marcy's? I mean, Marcy may have been coordinator for the event, but are we not all responsible for follow up? We need to do a better job of helping track follow-up visits. We've set two visits each week as our minimum. There is no reason we can't make three or four when our schedule allows."

Greg is nodding his head in affirmation and takes the lead by asking, "So, what can you as a team do to first rectify this and make sure these four families get visited this week? And second, what driving gauges can you build in to ensure timely follow up in the future?"

For the next five minutes, Greg leads the team in a discussion to resolve these issues and build in driving gauges for better follow up for future events. Satisfied that the team has come to a solid resolution and Susan has recorded the new follow-up measures, Greg turns the meeting back over to Pastor Tim.

The team resumes discussing statistics and reviewing their other driving gauges. In doing so, they determine they have, according to the parameters they set at the retreat, an additional seven families involved at a deeper level than before, including three new families enrolled in Bible study and other activities of the church. They are more than halfway to their goal in only three months. Thanks to the excitement created around the newly implemented visitation program and its emphasis, there is an average of fifteen people visiting in homes each week. That's an increase of 500 percent over the previous year. Attendance in Bible study and worship is rising, which is bringing an increase in giving as well. With the new focus on moving people to engagement, 4Cs is seeing more participation in events and mission activities. The church is in line to baptize more new converts than it has in at least eight years, and the overall atmosphere of the church is upbeat and joyful.

In addition to the structured and church sponsored activities and events, the staff is aware of 4Cs members intentionally engaged in developing relationships in community-related avenues: eight members are now in bowling leagues with the intent of building relationships with unchurched bowling league members. Five men started an outdoors sportsmen's monthly gathering and have seven fishermen and hunters involved from the community. Four women are scrapbooking with four other women in their community; three men, three women, and two teenagers attended the first golf clinic; and registration has almost doubled for the second one coming up the last weekend in September.

One 4Cs family, Dan Junna and his wife, Elizabeth, met in high school working in the drama club. Fourteen years later they are married with a nine year old daughter. Dan and Elizabeth still love the theater and with their daughter have joined a local theatrical group as a family with the distinct intent of building relationships to honor Christ and introduce other thespians to the saving grace of His gospel. One husband and wife couple from the theatrical group has joined Dan and Elizabeth on two occasions for worship in the first two months since making their commitment to serve Christ in this fashion.

In addition to these, testimonies are coming in from hairdressers, office workers, dental assistants, students, and others engaging in spirit-led relationship building.

Pastor Tim and the staff are pleased with these commitments. Though the number of people committed to developing these relationships is only a small portion of their church, the team realizes the number will grow, and in their prayer time, the staff prays each week for more believers to make the commitment. Pastor Tim Farling and Calvert City Community Church (4Cs) are realizing the vision of permeating the community and receiving results for their compassion and desire to build relationships that last and bring glory and honor to God.

Your church, ministry, or organization can make forward progress by following the process outlined in this book if the underlying principles are upheld. What are those principles? Unity, honesty, integrity, respect for all others, accountability, and of course, heart-felt, soul-bathed, Spirit-led prayer.

RECAP THE PROCESS

Let's recap the steps 4Cs set to implement and accomplish their process of being a Great Commission church for this one leg of their journey.

First they began leading the church in a particular prayer emphasis—not prayer as usual, but taking individuals in the church to a deeper level of prayer ministry. And this did not happen until the staff began doing the same in their own prayer time. Prayer must be an integral part at the beginning and throughout the process for strategic planning and implementation in your ministry.

The strategic planning began with determining an overarching goal (OG). From here to where by when? If we had only one thing to focus on for the next seven months (six months, year, your timetable), what should that be? *To move from twenty-nine families actively involved to forty families actively engaged in ministry and discipleship by the end of the year.* You need to determine the right "from here to where by when" for your ministry at this juncture in time.

The staff realized the vision conveyed to the church would need to be compelling for the members to want to get involved and be engaged in ministry to the community. The vision is your roadmap. It does not give photographs of your route or destination. But it does give you a charted idea of the path you will take.

The passion of your members and the ministries of the church will be your vehicle to drive you to your destination. A thorough reality check of your current ministries is crucial for you to get started right on your journey.

Your church's core values are the fuel that propels your vehicle toward your destination. A core values assessment should be completed before you set your overarching goal and before you begin your next leg of the journey. Your actions, as an individual and as a church body, are outward manifestations of what you truly and deeply believe. Without a proper understanding of your core values, you will be pouring the wrong type of fuel for your journey. For more on core values, see chapter four of Aubrey Malphurs' book *Advanced Strategic Planning*.[12]

Next, the 4Cs team determined their destination indicators. Destination indicators are those mile markers, street signs, and points of interest along the journey, telling you that you are on the right road and making progress toward your destination. The destination indicators do not necessarily help you reach your destination, but they will give you an indication of progress. Destination indicators are almost always reactors. By the time you reach a destination indicator, it is too late to make an adjustment for that part of the journey. However, you can make necessary adjustments for the remainder of your journey based on the knowledge you gain from your destination indicators.

Imagine on your journey you are using exit 57 as one of your destination indicators by planning to stop at a known restaurant for lunch. However, when you get off at exit 57 you find the restaurant is closed for business. In fact, there are no restaurants at exit 57. It is too late to not get off at exit 57. You have already made it to the exit. The only thing you can do is return to the highway and search for an open restaurant to fill your need.

Likewise if Vacation Bible School (VBS) is one of your destination indicators for your church journey, you are expecting VBS to give you certain information and results along the journey. You should always conduct debrief sessions following every event. However, what you learn in the debrief session cannot help you with this year's VBS. By the time you reach the debrief session, VBS is past. You can make plans for future events and next year's VBS based on what you learned. Destination indicators are more often reactors that can help you determine if you are on course and how to change for the future, but not for the indicator itself.

Following their determination of destination indicators, the team established the driving gauges for this particular leg of the journey. Driving gauges are with you throughout the journey and give you a quick analysis of the moment at hand—where you are right now on your journey. Driving gauges are important to your journey, assisting you in making decisions in the moment, what minor adjustments are needed today, like the driving gauges in your automobile: speed up, slow down, slight left curve of the steering wheel, when to brake, etc. While driving gauges are to be set to check at any point during the journey, you need a systematic approach to check your driving gauges as a team on a frequent basis. This systematic check should be as frequent as possible. Daily is best, and no longer than weekly. Some driving gauges may be based on weekly indicators and therefore cannot be gauged more frequently than weekly. The point is to have an automatic, built-in check system with friendly accountability.

Driving gauges are proactors. They help you see the here and now. Driving gauges give you the information needed to determine what immediate adjustments need to be made to keep you on course and moving in the right direction. The information to make a right turn at the next intersection gives you a proactive stance in staying true to your course on the journey.

At 4Cs, not everyone in the church jumped on board with the changes as they were first implemented. However, right away the church began seeing progress. The success came first because a vision was sparked in the pastor's heart. The staff and leadership were warmed by the burning embers of the pastor's vision and desire. The leaders then fanned the flame, stoking a fire that would warm the hearts of the members and light their way on this turn-around journey. Success in your church begins with a spark. Will you be the catalyst for that spark?

The journey was not over, only this particular leg of the journey. The first Tuesday of December was set aside for the staff and two other leaders from the church to get away for another planning retreat. This retreat was to work through similar exercises to strategically plan for the following year. This time the OG would be set for twelve months. The first session was committed to prayer and setting the new OG. The team in the following sessions set destination indicators and driving gauges for the next leg of the Calvert City Community Church journey. It was easily determined that this will become an annual retreat each year.

Set your mind to follow God's prescription for your ministry, and determine to join with other leaders in your church or organization to seek God's designed plan for the next leg of your journey as God's local body of believers. May each leg of your journey be one of God's progressive nature and blessings.

ENDNOTES

1. Yates, George. *Reaching the Summit: Avoiding and Reversing Decline in the Church.* Essence Publishing, 2012, chapter 7.

2. Yates, George. *Teaching That Bears Fruit.* Guardian Press, 2001, 2007.

3. Ibid.

4. Formulating Questions at www.soncare.net/reaching-the-summit-downloadable-resources.

5. Yates, *Reaching the Summit.*

6. Yates, *Teaching That Bears Fruit.*

7. Elridge, Daryl, Ed. *The Teaching Ministry of the Church.* 1995. Broadman and Holman. Chapter 11, "Planning to Teach," pg. 196.

8. Rainer, Thom S. and Ed Stetzer. *Transformational Church.* B&H Publishing, 2010, page 23.

9. Brown, Brene. "The Best Leaders are Vulnerable." Forbes.com. July 18, 2013.

10. Yates, *Teaching That Bears Fruit,* chapter 4.

11. Ibid, page 53.

12. Malphurs, Aubrey. *Advanced Strategic Planning.* Baker Books, 2006, chapter 4.